BOLD CARD PLAY:

Best Strategies for
Caribbean Stud, Let It Ride & Three-Card Poker

BY FRANK SCOBLETE

Bonus Books Inc.
Chicago, Illinois

02   01   00   99   98   5   4   3   2   1

Library of Congress Cataloging-in-Publication Data

Scoblete, Frank.
      Bold card play : best strategies for Caribbean stud, let it ride & three-card poker / by Frank Scoblete.
          p.   cm.
      Includes index.
      ISBN 1-56625-100-1 (alk. paper)
      1. Poker. 2. Gambling.   I. Title.
   GV1251.S34   1998
   795.41′2—dc21   98-15186
                                                                        CIP

Bonus Books, Inc.
160 East Illinois Street
Chicago, Illinois 60611

Printed in the Unites States of America

This book is dedicated to
Francis de Sales

and to the people who have helped to make me a household name
(at least in my household)

John Busam
Aaron Cohodes
Mike Epifanio
Catherine Jaeger
Alene Paone
Rudi Schiffer
Howard Schwartz
Cecil Suzuki

"He that lives upon hope will die fasting."

....Ben Franklin

Table of Contents

Acknowledgments

I had a lot of help in the writing of this book, especially from Shuffle Master Gaming, the developer of Let It Ride, and Prime Table Games, the developer of Three Card Poker. I would like to thank Jay Meilstrup, vice president of Game Development of Shuffle Master Gaming, and Patricia Marvel, advertising manager of Shuffle Master Gaming, and Derek Webb, president of Prime Table Games, each of whom spent quite a bit of time honestly answering my questions about their respective games.

In addition, I am grateful for the help that John Busam and Catherine Jaeger, the editors of *Midwest Gaming and Travel Magazine*, gave me in acquiring information on Caribbean Stud poker and, more importantly, for being such good friends. Thanks also in this respect to Michael Epifanio, managing editor of *Atlantic City Magazine*. A thank you to Adam Fine, managing editor, and Rick Greco, photography editor of *Casino Player Magazine* for their help; and to W. Michael Sunderman, publisher, and Lori Beth Sussman, editor, of *Jackpot Magazine* for their continued support. Special thanks to Rudi Schiffer, host of *The Goodtimes Show* and publisher of *Cigars and More*, whose help and friendship over the years have been greatly appreciated.

Of course, the beautiful and even-tempered A.P., my own personal editor, my friend, and my wife, always merits gratitude for her wise advice, which was no less crucial in bringing this book into being than it has been in bringing all my books to life. A thank you to my brother-in-law and writing partner, D.W. Paone, for allowing me to use him as an example in this book. Finally, to all the folks at Bonus Books, now and in the past, whose combined efforts have helped to make me a success...a really BIG thank you!

1

Why the New Games? And Why They're Catching On!

The casinos in America have always done quite well with the table games they already have, yet today they are constantly experimenting with new table games. Why? When I asked casino executives this question, the standard answer went something like this: "We want to give our customers more choices, more ways to win, more games to play. We also want to give our slot players an opportunity to play table games."

There is a modicum of truth even in the obfuscations that pass for responses of spokespeople for the casino (or any) industry to pointed questions, and an analysis of the above generic statement as to why the casinos are offering new games reveals a dawning truth. In truth, the casinos *do* want to offer their slot players the opportunity to play table games. In truth, the casinos *do* want to offer their players more choices and more ways to win (which is *newspeak* for "new ways to lose").

But why?

Because it is also true that people tend to play for much bigger stakes at table games and that table-game players tend to come to casinos with much bigger bankrolls than do slot players. Table-game players also lose more, per person, than do slot players. There is much more money to feast on for the casino banqueters if they can bring their slot players to the tables and devour them pocketbook and purse.

Another factor also operates in the attempt to get slot players to partake in the tables in addition to the higher stakes, bigger bankrolls, and greater losses. Today's casinos are facing massive competition in their slot marketing and as a result more and more casinos are offering better and better paybacks on their machines and better deals for their slot club members. A one-dollar slot machine paying back 98 percent—as we now find in many casinos across the country as I write this—can be played in such a leisurely fashion that a player's expected loss could be almost minuscule in terms of real money. As the slot machines become better bets for the players, they become troublesome for the casinos' bottom lines. At the tables, it is usually the dealer who controls the pace of play (albeit some players can and should slow down the action) and that pace is as fast as a given game will allow. Slot machines are rarely played at breakneck speed (except in tournaments) and smart slot players have learned to pace themselves to allow their money to last for the expected duration of their sessions and stays.

If we compared a dollar slot machine returning 98 percent and a table game with a minimum bet of five or ten dollars returning 98 percent (each having a house edge, therefore, of 2 percent), it would be no secret that the table game would make much more money for the casino because that two percent edge was working on a lot more cash. You would also notice that while the table minimum of a given game might be thus-and-such, many people bet much more than the minimum. In fact, even players who start out betting the minimum sometimes find themselves increasing their bets, often to try to get back what they have lost or to capitalize on a hot streak that they hope will continue. A table-game player can increase the size of his or her bets without going to another table (and wasting precious time) while a slot player can only play the denomination of machine that he or she is on. If a slot player wants to go to a different denomination of play, he or she has to get up and physically move to another machine. When slot players are in transit, they aren't making money for the casinos. In the casino, time is money. It's the $E=MC^2$ of Lady Luck.

Yes, the casinos are, therefore, telling the truth when they say their new table games are being offered in an attempt to get some slot players to the tables. But what about the players who are already at the tables? Do the casinos want to give their other table games competition by luring players from one table to another?

You bet they do!

Here's why.

The top four traditional table games are blackjack, craps, roulette, and baccarat (or mini-baccarat). They've been around for years and years. Baccarat has a house edge of slightly more than one percent for its two major bets. Played properly both blackjack and craps can yield edges hovering at the .5 percent mark (and sometimes lower). Although roulette has a rather large house edge of 5.26 percent on the double-zero or American wheel and 2.70 percent on the single-zero or European wheel, the game is quite leisurely with not that many decisions per hour. Here's something to memorize: a smaller percentage of many more decisions usually equals much more money for the casinos than a larger percentage of many fewer decisions. The more the roulette ball spins around the wheel before dropping into a pocket, the less money the casinos actually make. Time is money redux.

If you take a look at each of the popular new table games that I am covering in this book, you will note that not one has a house edge of less than 2 percent and that Caribbean Stud, the slowest of the three games, comes in at over 5 percent! (This assumes that the player is using the Bold Card Play strategies. The edges are much higher if players don't use Bold Card Play but some invented strategies of their own.)

Yet, these three games are catching on like wild fire with some slot players, and table-game players, and for good reasons. All three are more or less attractive games to play. First, because the strategies are easier to learn than are the strategies for the various types of blackjack games. Second, because the strategies the players employ do have real consequences on how much they can expect to win and lose over time. It isn't all dumb luck. (Why is luck dumb? Why can't it be smart?) Players enjoy matching wits with the casino and these three games give them an opportunity to flex some gray matter.

However, unlike blackjack, the choices at Caribbean Stud, Let It Ride and Three Card Poker are made privately. The other players don't care how you play your cards because your decisions have no bearing on their hands. Many blackjack players persist in believing that the bad play of other players affects their own expectations of winning and these same blackjack players are often not adverse to commenting scathingly on your strategy for playing the hands, or your general intelligence, or your genetic makeup should you violate their concept of optimum play. Despite the fact that computer studies have shown time and again that the play of other blackjack players' hands has little bearing on the long-range outcomes for you, most blackjack players do not believe this. In fact, many blackjack players are quick to criticize other players, either by word or wince, and this can scare off novices and their wallets. The casinos know this and are attempting to alleviate the "critics corner" that is blackjack with more player-muting table games.

With Caribbean Stud, Let It Ride or Three Card Poker, the other players don't know and don't care what you do—just as most slot players don't care what other slot players do at their machines and most craps players don't care what bets other craps players are making. And certainly these new games please the casinos because, even with the best strategies that I'll reveal in this book, it is impossible to mathematically overcome the house edge in any of them as one can turn the tables in blackjack. Certainly, we can reduce the house edge by a great degree (and we will), we can play smart (and we will), but ultimately the math will take its toll (and, sadly, it will)—but cheer up, with the strategies in this book we will give the mighty casinos a bold fight in their new games.

There is a third very good reason why Caribbean Stud, Let It Ride, and Three Card Poker are catching on. Each game offers better than one-to-one payouts for premium hands and two games, Caribbean Stud and Let It Ride, actually offer the potential to win those Hefty-bag-sized bundles of cash if luck should strike. These games have plugged into (or were deliberately plugged into) the dominant player dream that envisions going for the gusto as the preferred way to approach casino games. With bonus hands and jackpot features, the new games also appeal to the slot players who are used to dreaming of big returns for small investments.

Yet, something has to give when games are structured to have such features and, generally speaking, the better the bonus payoff, the fewer the absolute number of wins for the player. In blackjack, the player wins about 44 percent of the time, in craps (on good bets) the player can win close to 50 percent of the time, and in baccarat the player wins a shade under half his decisions on one bet (the *player* bet) and is taxed on another bet (the *bank* bet) that actually wins more than half the time. On the even-money bets at roulette, the player wins slightly less than 50 percent of the time as well. In contrast, Let It Ride sees players winning less than one-fourth of the time! Of course, when the players do win, it is often for greater than a one-to-one payoff. And that is just like the slots. You don't win anything close to half your spins on a slot machine but of the spins that you do win, some are for rather large returns. That's a thrilling prospect for many players and is one of the reasons for slot play's popularity.

Fourth and finally, Caribbean Stud, Let it Ride, and Three Card Poker are all based on variations of a game most casino gamblers are familiar with—traditional poker. Thus, the scope of the games, including the ranking of the various possible hands, is already within the consciousness of the players. Most players have played poker or, at the very least, know the generalities of the game. There is almost a Jungian collective-poker-consciousness that the new games can plug into. The new games are also plugging into the fact that many kitchen poker players are too timid (and perhaps too smart) to enter the shark-infested poker rooms of the casinos but would be ready, willing, able and even anxious to play a variation of poker at a player-friendly table. In addition, the casinos have seen the spectacular success of video poker and have created table games that piggyback on that success. Indeed, the new table games are somewhat reminiscent of video poker, although they are even easier to play expertly. Many video poker games have between 18 and 40 discreet strategy decisions to make—some have even more—while none of the new games in this book have anything remotely near the sheer number and variety of decisions you have to make at video poker.

In conclusion, we can see that the casinos are offering these new games based on variations of the already-familiar poker to lure players away from better paying games such as blackjack, craps and baccarat, where house edges are around 1 percent or less. The new games have house edges that start at just over 2 percent and climb upwards of 5 percent. When we say the house has an edge of, say, 2 percent, what we are really saying is that for every $100 you bet at this game, in the long run you can expect to lose two dollars. The new games do require a certain expertise however, but not the level of skill that blackjack entails, and the best strategies are comparatively simple to learn and apply in real casino conditions. The new games also plug into the dominant player psychology that has us wanting to win a lot of money—we want bonus hands and jackpots for our gambling thrills—and the new games give us these.

Why have Caribbean Stud, Let It Ride, and Three Card Poker caught on when other games such as Casino War, Red Dog, Russian Roulette, and Pokette with similar attributes have failed, some miserably? You do get to make some choices in some of the aforementioned games and those choices certainly do have an impact on your chances of winning and losing. Strange as it may seem, players I spoke to perceived Caribbean Stud, Let It Ride, and Three-Card Poker as offering them a decent chance to take home the money. Most of the players I spoke to made a point of saying that they had had enough winning experiences, some quite lucrative in the short run, with one or another of these games to make them want to continue playing it in the future. Almost no players I spoke to were ahead over an extended period of time but, conversely, almost no players I spoke with played anything resembling the correct strategies for their hands on any of the games. The combination of the house edge and their poor play was dooming them to greater losses than would otherwise be the case.

Bold Card Play is being written to give those players who want the best chance of winning at Caribbean Stud, Let It Ride, and Three Card Poker, the best *possible* strategies, which are also the best *practical* strategies for doing so. Unlike a new game such as Russian Roulette—which one shift boss at the Maxim characterized as: "A game where I never saw a player win a bet!"—all three games in this book offer a greater or lesser opportunity to make the player some money if played properly. The Bold Card Play strategies are the best strategies to play. Coupled with the money-management systems that I recommend in the upcoming chapters, they will help to cut the house edge and increase your chances to win. That's a fact. Lady Luck has a tendency to more frequently favor the person who courts her with a bit of finesse—that's another fact.

To use a boxing analogy. Good big men invariably beat good little men for a variety of reasons. The good big man can take a bigger punch and deliver a bigger punch than can a good little man. In most casino games, the casinos are good big men but the players are *bad* little men. The players haven't got a prayer in other words, and that's why they get knocked out so often. Although the Bold Card Play strategies in this book can't make you a good big man fighting a good big man in these three new casino games, they can help you to become a great *medium* man—and *great* medium men (and women) can beat the big boys every so often.

So, now, let's get into the ring with Lady Luck, shall we?

2
Hierarchy of Poker Hands

All the new card games discussed in this book are based on the great all-American game of stud poker. Although all the games will be individually discussed and analyzed in chapters of their own, the information in this chapter is a necessary foundation. At first I was not going to write this chapter because (I thought) everyone in America knows the ranking of poker hands—right? Well, my brother-in-law and script-writing partner, D.W. Paone, just said to me: "So what beats what in these new games?"

"What?"

"I said what beats what in these new games?" he reiterated.

"What do you mean what beats what?" I replied. "It's just regular poker hands."

"I've never played poker," he said.

"Come on," I said.

"No, I never did," he insisted.

"How is that possible?" I asked.

"I don't know many people who have played poker," he said.

"You're kidding," I said.

"No."

"How can it be that you don't know what poker hands are?"

"I told you I never played it."

"You mean you don't know what a flush is?" I asked.

"Yeah, your face turns red," he said.
"Very witty," I replied.
"So you tell me, what's a flush?"
So I told him.

What I didn't tell him, however, was that a flush would have been on my face had I not included this chapter. So I stood corrected. I assumed everyone would know what beats what at poker but not everyone does. So, this chapter is for you D.W.

The Number of Cards in a Hand:

In Caribbean Stud and Let It Ride, you judge your hands based on five cards. This is a traditional poker hand and just about all varieties of regulation poker pits the five card hand of one player against five card hands of other players. In Three Card Poker you judge your hand based on three cards. Although you are not competing against other players in any of these games, I have given the rules for hands that seemingly tie. In the cases of Caribbean Stud and Three Card Poker, you are competing with the dealer and the rules will apply to those times when you and the dealer have the same high hand. Here's an example of what I'm talking about. If I have two Aces and two Kings and D.W. had two Aces and two Kings, we would then compare our fifth card to see who won. If I had a Jack and D.W. had a 7, I would win. If we both had Jacks, the hand would be a tie or push.

Hierarchy of Cards - Highest to Lowest:

Ace	10	5
King	9	4
Queen	8	3
Jack	7	2
	6	

(An ace may also be used as a "one" in the making of hands called "straights")

Poker Rankings of Five Card Hands

1. Royal Flush: Ace, King, Queen, Jack, 10 of the same suit.

2. Straight Flushes: five cards in order of the same suit.

    Hierarchy: King, Queen, Jack, 10, 9 of same suit
    Queen, Jack, 10, 9, 8 of same suit
    Jack, 10, 9, 8, 7 of the same suit
    10, 9, 8, 7, 6 of the same suit
    9, 8, 7, 6, 5 of the same suit
    8, 7, 6, 5, 4 of the same suit
    7, 6, 5, 4, 3 of the same suit
    6, 5, 4, 3, 2 of the same suit
    5, 4, 3, 2, Ace of the same suit

3. Four-of-a-kind: four cards of the same denomination.

    Hierarchy: Four Aces
    Four Kings
    Four Queens
    Four Jacks
    Four 10s
    Four 9s
    Four 8s
    Four 7s
    Four 6s
    Four 5s
    Four 4s
    Four 3s
    Four 2s (also known as deuces)

4. Full House: three of one denomination and two of another denomination.

    Hierarchy: Three Aces with any pair.
    Three Kings with any pair.
    Three Queens with any pair.
    Three Jacks with any pair.

Three 10s with any pair.
Three 9s with any pair.
Three 8s with any pair.
Three 7s with any pair.
Three 6s with any pair.
Three 5s with any pair.
Three 4s with any pair.
Three 3s with any pair.
Three 2s with any pair.

In the case of two full houses competing, the full house with the highest three card portion wins.

5. Flush: any five cards of the same suit.

   Hierarchy: When two (or more) flushes compete with each
               other, the flush with the highest card wins. If
               flushes have the same high card, then the second
               highest cards of each are compared and so forth.

6. Straight: any five cards in order of denomination.

   Hierarchy: Ace, King, Queen, Jack, 10 of different suits.
               King, Queen, Jack, 10, 9 of different suits.
               Queen, Jack, 10, 9, 8 of different suits.
               Jack, 10, 9, 8, 7 of different suits.
               10, 9, 8, 7, 6 of different suits.
               9, 8, 7, 6, 5 of different suits.
               8, 7, 6, 5, 4 of different suits.
               7, 6, 5, 4, 3 of different suits.
               6, 5, 4, 3, 2 of different suits.
               5, 4, 3, 2, Ace of different suits.

7. Three-of-a-kind: Three cards of the same denomination.

   Hierarchy: Three Aces with any other cards.
               Three Kings with any other cards.
               Three Queens with any other cards.
               Three Jacks with any other cards.

Three 10s with any other cards.
Three 9s with any other cards.
Three 8s with any other cards.
Three 7s with any other cards.
Three 6s with any other cards.
Three 5s with any other cards.
Three 3s with any other cards.
Three 2s with any other cards.

8. Two Pair: two of one denomination and two of another denomination.

    Hierarchy: Based on card rankings, the hand with the highest pair wins. For example, Scobe has two Aces and two Deuces, while D.W. has two Kings and two Queens—Scobe [that's my nickname] wins because Aces beat Kings. If Scobe and D. W. both have two Aces and two Kings, then the fifth card's ranking determines the outcome. Thus, if D.W. has a Jack and Scobe has a 10, D.W. would win the hand (I had to let him win one!). If we both have identical hands, it's a tie.

9. One Pair: two of one denomination and any three other cards.

    Hierarchy: Two Aces with any other cards.
    Two Kings with any other cards.
    Two Queens with any other cards.
    Two Jacks with any other cards.
    Two 10s with any other cards.
    Two 9s with any other cards.
    Two 8s with any other cards.
    Two 7s with any other cards.
    Two 6s with any other cards.
    Two 5s with any other cards.
    Two 4s with any other cards.
    Two 3s with any other cards.
    Two 2s with any other cards.

Note that if two players have the same pair, the highest of the other three cards is the determining factor. If that card is the same, the next highest card determines the winner and so forth.

10. High Cards

    Hierarchy: Follows the hierarchy of rank. Note that if the highest card is a tie, the next highest card determines the winner and so forth. Thus, Ace, Jack, 7, 4, 2 beats Ace, Jack, 5, 4, 3 because a 7 beats a 5.

POKER RANKINGS of Three Card Hands

1.   Straight Flush: Three cards of the same suit in order of denomination.

    Hierarchy: Ace, King, Queen of same suit.
                  King, Queen, Jack of same suit.
                  Queen, Jack, 10 of same suit.
                  Jack, 10, 9 of same suit.
                  10, 9, 8 of same suit.
                  9, 8, 7 of same suit.
                  8, 7, 6 of same suit.
                  7, 6, 5 of same suit.
                  6, 5, 4 of same suit.
                  5, 4, 3 of same suit.
                  4, 3, 2 of same suit.
                  3, 2, Ace of same suit.

2.   Three-of-a kind: Three cards of the same denomination.

    Hierarchy: Three Aces
                  Three Kings
                  Three Queens
                  Three Jacks
                  Three 10s
                  Three 9s
                  Three 8s
                  Three 7s

Three 6s
Three 5s
Three 4s
Three 3s
Three 2s

3. Straight: Any three cards in order of denomination.

Hierarchy: Ace, King, Queen of different suits.
King, Queen, Jack of different suits.
Queen, Jack, 10 of different suits.
Jack, 10, 9 of different suits.
10, 9, 8 of different suits.
9, 8, 7 of different suits.
8, 7, 6, of different suits.
7, 6, 5 of different suits.
6, 5, 4 of different suits.
5, 4, 3 of different suits.
4, 3, 2 of different suits
3, 2, Ace of different suits

4. Flush: Any three cards of one suit.

Hierarchy: When two or more flushes compete, the one with
the highest denomination card wins. If two or more
hands share the same high card, then the next highest card is compared and so forth.

5. Pair: Two cards of the same rank.

Hierarchy: Based on ranking of cards—two Aces are highest,
two Deuces are lowest. In the case of exact
pairs competing, the third card determines the winner based on ranking of cards—Ace high, Deuce low.

6. Non-Pair Hands: Winners are determined by comparing the highest card of the three. If two or more players have the same high card, the second highest card is compared and so on.

You'll note that on three-card hands, there is a reversal in the value of three-of-a-kind, straight and flush because it is harder to get three-of-a-kind on three cards than on five cards but much easier to get a flush on three cards than on five cards. The straight is also much harder to get on three cards than is a flush.

TERMINOLOGY

Some terms might be unfamiliar to the non-poker player. I asked D.W. Paone what "drawing to an inside straight" meant and he said: "Sending a painting to a guy in prison who isn't gay?"

No.

An "inside straight" is a straight that can only be made by drawing a card that fits within the highest and lowest denomination of the cards you have. For example, I have Ace, Jack, 10 and I need to draw two cards. To get my straight, I must draw a Queen and a King, which fit "inside" the cards I have. Sometimes this can be called a "spot" draw as you are looking to get a card to fill a specific "spot." With four cards, a player with Ace, 2, 3, 5 is looking to fill the "spot" left vacant by the 4.

An "outside" straight means you are trying to get a card that completes the straight on the outside of the denominations. For example, I have Ace, King, Queen, Jack but I need the 10 to get the straight.

An "open-ended" straight is one where you can fill in either end in a few ways. Let us say you have 7, 8, 9. It's clear that both ends of the straight are open to completion. In fact, there are a number of ways the straight can be completed. You can get a 10 and a Jack. You can get a 5 and a 6. You can also get a 6 and a 10. With four cards such as 7, 8, 9, 10 you need either a 6 or a Jack to complete the straight.

How New Games Differ from Standard Poker

In standard poker, you are competing against other players and the player with the best hand *doesn't* always win the pot. Good players who have mastered the art of the bluff will often scare away other players from the pot—players who actually had, or were working on, better hands. No such situation exists in the new games. Although in Caribbean Stud some writers use the term "bluffing" to describe a player staying in on certain losing hands in the hopes that the dealer will not qualify, it is not the equivalent of real bluffing. In reality, staying in on bad hands in the hopes the dealer won't qualify at Caribbean Stud is just called *staying in on bad hands in the hopes the dealer won't qualify* (read Franklin's quote on hope again!). You aren't scaring the dealer out of the game, you are just making a big mistake in the playing of your hands. It's also called *dumb* play.

The skills that a good poker player needs are many and diverse. Some may even be genetic. A good poker player has to have a knowledge of the odds of making any hand at any given time and what impact those odds have on the money in the pot. He has to know the psychology of the other players and he has to know himself. He has to be flexible in his playing strategy and often he must alter it to suit his opponents. He also has to have nerves of steal, a killer instinct, and a stoic philosophy about money.

In the new table games, knowledge of the odds is not necessary as long as you have memorized the correct play of each hand you get. Like blackjack, you can become a skillful player without any concept of the math behind your decisions. It's just memorization. There is no flexibility in your play whatsoever. Play the Bold Card Play strategies and you have the best chance to win. Simple dictum. Simple truth.

The Bold Card Play strategies that follow are the best practical strategies for playing the new games. These strategies will reduce the house edge—sometimes markedly—from other strategies that you may have been using. Some players playing these new games are giving the casino edges in the double digits. Play the Bold Card Play strategies and you won't have to worry about being one of them.

3
Bold Card Play Strategy for Caribbean Stud

For years the islands of the Caribbean have been offering relatively awful blackjack and craps games, as have the "love" boats that often bring their unwitting but eager pilgrims to the island paradises' ports of call. The islands also offered their own games, which for gamblers were isles of despair. Games played on the cruise ships made the "love boats" more often than not the ships of fools. One such game is Caribbean Stud, which has recently stormed onto the mainland (circa 1993) and, like a hurricane, has blown through many an unwary gambler's bankroll. Like any card game that requires players to make decisions, Caribbean Stud rewards those players who make the right choices (they lose less) and punishes those players who make the wrong choices (they lose more). Losing more or less is of vital concern to anyone who enters a casino be it on boat or island or mainland.

THE RULES OF THE GAME

The game of Caribbean Stud is offered on a blackjack-like table and, as in blackjack, all players play against the house. Most tables seat up to seven players. A standard deck of 52 playing cards is used.

Most Caribbean Stud games that I have come across use a shuffle machine in order to keep the hands flowing with as little delay as possible between decisions.

There are two betting squares in front of each player—one is labeled *ante* and the other is labeled *bet*. The *bet* area looks like a treasure chest just bursting with gold coins—which is, of course, the psychological inducement to bet the *bet*. The *ante* is the rectangular area. Atop the *ante* on the layout is a side bet—the jackpot—that is made by dropping a one dollar chip in the jackpot slot. When a player opts to place a dollar coin in the jackpot, he becomes eligible to hit the progressive jackpot (or a percentage thereof) that increases with each hand played. The side jackpot bet is strictly optional and has nothing to do with the winning and losing of hands. Like progressive slot machines, each Caribbean Stud table has a progressive meter that informs the player where the jackpot is at any given moment. For some players, this jackpot feature is a major inducement to play the game.

The game begins with the players putting a bet in the *ante* square and, if they wish (death wish, actually, as we shall see), they can put a dollar in the jackpot bet. When the players who are going to make the jackpot bet have done so, the dealer presses a button and the dollar coin drops into the slot much the way an actor drops through a trap door on a stage. A red light will now indicate which jackpot slots have received coins.

Now the dealer deals five cards face down to each player. Unlike blackjack, you are not allowed to show your cards to the other players. The dealer also deals himself five cards, the last of which is dealt face up. The players check their cards.

They now have two choices to make:

Choice One: They can play out their hands if they think they'll be able to beat the dealer.

Choice Two: They can surrender their hands and lose their *antes* if they think they can't beat the dealer.

Figure One:
Caribbean Stud Layout

If they decide to play out their hands (sometimes referred to as "calling the dealer"), they must place a bet that is *double* their *ante* in the *bet* square. Once the players have made their respective decisions, the players put all their cards face down on the table. The dealer will now scoop up the *ante* bets from all the players who dropped out. This done, the dealer turns over his remaining four cards and makes the best possible poker hand out of them.

The one caveat is that the dealer must have at least an Ace-King in his hand for the game to be fully decided. This is called *qualifying*. If the dealer fails to have a hand that is Ace-King or better, meaning he fails to qualify, he pays off the *antes* and he pushes on the *bets*.

Pushing on a bet merely means that neither the player nor the house has won. In this case, the player takes back the *bet* wager. If the dealer qualifies with a hand of Ace-King (or better), then all the players' hands are judged against it. If the player cannot beat the dealer's hand, the player loses both his *ante* and his *bet*. If the player beats the dealer, the *ante* is paid off at even money (you get one dollar for every dollar you bet), while the *bet* is paid off at house odds as follows:

Winning Hand	Bonus Payout Table
Ace-King	1 to 1
One Pair	1 to 1
Two Pair	2 to 1
Three-of-a-kind	3 to 1
Straight	4 to 1
Flush	5 to 1
Full House	7 to 1
Four-of-a-kind	20 to 1
Straight Flush	50 to 1
Royal Flush	100 to 1

Keep in mind that if the dealer doesn't qualify, you don't win the *bet* bonus—no matter how good your hand is. This is the most frustrating part of the game. You also don't win a bonus if the dealer beats your hand. If the player and the dealer have the same hand, then the remaining cards in the hand are compared and whoever has the high card wins. On rare occasions, all the remaining cards are the same. In that case, the hand is a true push and no money is exchanged.

However, if the player originally opted for the jackpot side bet, certain select hands will win a bonus award, up to and including the jackpot itself, regardless of what the dealer has and regardless of whether the dealer qualified. Although there is a range of bonus awards and jackpots, depending upon the casino or state you're playing in, the following is a relatively representative example of the payoffs.

Hand	Progressive Bonus
one pair	none
two pair	none
three of a kind	none
straight	none
flush	$50
full house	$75
four of a kind	$100
straight flush	10 percent of the progressive jackpot
royal flush	100 percent of the progressive jackpot

There are two more caveats to be aware of in Caribbean Stud in addition to the necessity for the dealer to qualify. These are:

1. You must tell the dealer you have won a jackpot bonus when he fails to qualify.

After you have put your cards face down on the table and called the dealer ("calling" means that you are competing against the dealer's hand), if the dealer subsequently does not qualify, he will not turn over your cards when collecting them. If you have placed a coin in the jackpot slot, you must inform the dealer that you have won a bonus, otherwise, he'll take your cards and there goes your winning jackpot combination—right into the shuffle machine!

2. Be aware of the maximum payout as stated on the game card at the table.

Many casinos limit the maximum payout that they'll give on a winning call bet. (That's another way of saying a winning *bet* bet.) Let us say that you *ante* $200 and then place a $400 *call* bet. On a winning straight flush, you are mathematically entitled to a payoff of $20,000 for the *call bet* ($400 X 50 = $20,000) and $200 for your *ante*. However, if the maximum that the table will pay out is $10,000, then that's all you'll receive as payment for your *call bet*. The casino is really hammering you if you make bets that can't be paid off at the listed odds because you've exceeded the table limit. So before you place any *antes*, be aware of what you should win *should you win* and make sure that the casino will pay it off. If you don't do that, you might have the worst case of good luck you could imagine!

The Best Strategy for Caribbean Stud

Caribbean Stud can be approached with a simple, easy-to-learn, easy-to-execute-in-a-casino strategy that will yield the house an edge of approximately 5.3 percent against the player. Or it can be approached with a convoluted, incredibly complex, almost impossible-to-learn-and-execute-in-a-casino optimum strategy—or *perfect* strategy—that will yield the house an edge of 5.2 percent against the player.

Yes, the casinos have made this particular game player proof—except in rare cases where the progressive jackpot is in the stratosphere or, in even rarer cases, where the pit is so lax that the players can all show their cards to each other in order to determine with a decent degree of probability what the dealer will likely have under his up card.

Sans that, the game can't be beaten.

However, improper strategy, the "I know what I'm doing and don't tell me any different" strategy, can give the house edges ranging from 7 percent and higher. Obviously, Caribbean Stud, with those high house percentages, is not the optimum casino game to play—regardless of what type of strategy you employ. The Bold Card Play approach takes the simplest way by promulgating the easier-to-use-in-a-real-casino strategy as opposed to the *perfect* strategy, which is a perfectly gruesome strategy to attempt to learn. Still, for those of you who wish to cut the house edge down another fraction by spending countless months (perhaps, years) attempting to memorize the perfect strategy, I recommend Stanley Ko's excellent booklet titled *Mastering the Game of Caribbean Stud Poker*.

Therefore, the best realistic strategy for Caribbean Stud is the Bold Card Play Five-Star approach:

1. Fold every hand that is below Ace-King in value against every dealer upcard. (Thus, if you have a King-Queen or a Queen-Jack surrender the *ante*.)

2. Bet an Ace-King hand—if your hand contains the dealer's upcard. (Thus, you have, say, A-K-7-3-2 and the dealer's upcard is 7, you place the call bet. However, if you have A-K-7-3-2 and the dealer's upcard is not 7 or 3 or 2, you give up your *ante*.)

3. Bet all Ace-King hands with Jack-8-3 or better against every dealer upcard.

4. Bet every pair or better against all dealer upcards.

5. Do not put up a jackpot bet.

This Five-Star Bold Card Play strategy is the best *possible* and *practical* strategy to employ in a casino against Carbbean Stud poker.

A Sample Round of Play

Now that we know the strategy, let's play a practice round of Caribbean Stud. We have six players at the table: K. Lewless, Willy Win, D.W., the beautiful A.P., you, and me.

The dealer tells us to place our bets. K. Lewless, Willy Win, and D.W. place jackpot side bets (D.W. rarely listens to anyone's advice, so why would he listen to me?). The dealer now deals each of us five cards and himself five cards. He flips over a Jack. K. Lewless has a Queen, ten, six, three, and two. He smiles knowingly. "Dealer's gonna not qualify," he says, showing some missing teeth, as he slides a *bet* wager out.

Willy Win has a King, nine, eight, seven, four. He surrenders his hand and grumbles that the game is obviously fixed as he's lost every time he's played it. He then asks for another marker.

D.W. looks at his hand. He has a pair of threes. Despite the fact that he has a copy of the Bold Card Play strategy in front of him (which, by the way, I have photocopied for him free of charge), he surrenders his hand.

"I have a feeling," he says.

"It's probably gas," I reply.

The beautiful A.P. has a bit of a dilemma with her hand. She has an Ace, King, Jack, five and three. She checks her Bold Card Play strategy, notes that she has an Ace-King hand that contains the dealer's upcard, and she places a *bet* wager.

You now check your hand. You have three sevens and two eights—a full house! You will be paid seven to one if you beat the dealer (which you will, since I have fixed the game in your favor because you bought this book). You quickly put down a *bet* wager.

I now look at my hand. A royal flush! (Hey, I'm creating this scenario, so I might as well fantasize a little.) I place a *bet* wager.

The dealer now turns over his cards. He has a Queen, Jack, nine, two, two—a pair of twos! He qualifies! You win, I win, A.P. loses, D.W. bows his head in shame (he should have followed the right strategy so don't feel sorry for him), Willy Win fidgets, K. Lewless guffaws.

Caribbean Stud Video Poker

There is a new video poker version of Caribbean Stud that is also being offered to the machine-playing public, although whether it will catch on with the casino players is open to question. The video version of the game is played the same way as the table-game version.

Most Caribbean Stud video poker machines can take up to 33 coins. You press the *ante* button for as many coins as you are going to play. Unlike most video poker games, you do not have to bet full coin to be eligible for the jackpot. As in the table game, you just put another coin in the progressive jackpot by pressing the button for that particular option.

Once your coins are in, you press the *deal* button and the machine will deal you five cards face-up at the bottom of the screen and it will deal itself five cards (four face down and one face up) on top. To *call* the dealer, you simply press the *bonus* button. The strategy for the video poker version of the game is the same as for the table game version, although the payout chart is somewhat different. You will note that I am expressing the bonus payout as "for" instead of "to" in the following chart as in 4 *for* 1 as opposed to 4 *to* 1. Whenever you see the word "for" in a payoff, it indicates that the *return* of your original bet is a part of that payout. If you are paid $4 *to* $1, you get $4 *plus* your bet back, which equals $5; however, if you are paid $4 *for* $1, you only get $4 back, which means a $3 win plus your original $1 bet. It's a tricky way the casinos have of making you think that you're actually getting more value for the payoff than is actually the case.

Hand	Bonus Payouts:
Ace-King	2 for 1
One Pair	2 for 1
Two Pair	2 for 1
Three-of-a-kind	4 for 1
Straight	6 for 1
Flush	10 for 1
Full House	15 for 1
Four-of-a-kind	100 for 1
Straight Flush	200 for 1
Royal Flush	1000 for 1

Although at first it looks as if you're getting a much better deal on the video version of the game because of the bigger payouts on the straights through the royal flushes, the fact that Two-Pair is only paying what Ace-King and One-Pair pays reduces the benefit of the superior paybacks on the other hands. Still, the Bold Card Play strategy on the video version will reduce the house edge to 5.1 percent because of the better payouts. Don't get too excited about such a reduction because you will play many, many more hands at the machine than you ever will play at the table. Despite the fact that your bets are likely to be smaller on each machine decision doesn't mean that you'll lose less overall, as the extra hands (some players estimate up to 300 hands-per-hour can be played!) could easily result in much *greater* losses.

Another unique feature of the video-version is a two-level progressive jackpot feature. You receive the regular jackpot for a royal flush, just as in regular Caribbean Stud, but it also offers a special monster jackpot for a royal flush in sequence. Don't hold your breath too long over this reward because the chance that you (or anyone else) will get it is approximately 39,000,000 to one!

Here are the common payouts for the progressive jackpot side bet on the video version of Caribbean Stud. Remember that the progressive side bet is paid off no matter who wins the actual play of the hands. Again you get back your original bet as a part of the bonus.

Hand	Number of Coins
Two Pair	1 coin
Three-of-a-kind	5 coins
Straight	25 coins
Flush	50 coins
Full House	100 coins
Four-of-a-kind	400 coins
Straight Flush	2,000 coins
Royal Flush	100% of first progressive jackpot
Sequential Royal	100% of monster progressive jackpot

QUESTIONS AND ANSWERS

Here are some of the most frequently-asked questions concerning Caribbean Stud. In doing research for this book, I spoke to 167 Caribbean Stud players in Las Vegas and Atlantic City. Strangely, only eight of these had ever read anything on the subject. In addition, during my frequent talks at book stores, libraries and other organizations, many people have asked me questions about Caribbean Stud and all the new games. I have included some of those here as well. Hopefully, this section will answer any questions that you might have.

I read in a magazine that the edge for Caribbean Stud was only 2.6 percent. Yet you state that it is 5.3 percent. What gives?

There are two basic ways to figure out the edge at Caribbean Stud—each yielding a different percentage while still yielding almost the exact same amount earned by the casino. This situation also exists in Let It Ride, where two figures also tend to be cited: 3.5 percent and 2.8 percent. In Caribbean Stud, the 5.3 percent figure is the amount the casino will win in the long run from the "ante" bet and the 2.6 percent is what the casino can expect to win on the "average" bet or unit wagered, which takes into consideration those times when the player raises his bets. In Let It Ride the 2.8 percent figure includes those times when you let all your bets ride and the 3.5 figure represents the advantage per hand.

Why shouldn't I put up a jackpot bet? After all, one of the reasons that I play Caribbean Stud is to win big bucks.

In my book *Guerrilla Gambling: How to Beat the Casinos at Their Own Games!*, I had estimated that the jackpot would have to reach $150,000 to make it a worthwhile bet. I was defining worthwhile as either the player having a slightly positive expectation (or a *slightly* negative expectation) when the jackpot got to that level. Since the publication of *Guerrilla Gambling*, new research (largely done by Stanley Ko) has indicated that I was somewhat off the mark (to be generous, I missed the broadside of the barn!), as Ko estimates that the jackpot has to reach almost $344,000 for a $5 *ante* player to have a slightly positive expectation (for a $10+ *ante* player it has to be even higher!).

I have never seen a jackpot that high in any casino. Ko reports in his excellent booklet *Mastering the Game of Caribbean Stud Poker* (Gambology Press) that the highest jackpot ever recorded was $660,000 on the Empress II riverboat in Illinois. Ko also states that he has personally seen a jackpot at the Las Vegas Hilton in the vicinity of $440,000. In my many sojourns in the casino kingdoms of Atlantic City and Las Vegas, I have seen jackpots in the $100,000 to $130,000 range on some occasions so I'm not too worried about players finding many $150,000 jackpots to bet on if they follow my original advice—whew! Although there might be rare times when the jackpot bet could be considered, overall it is an awful bet. Most of the casinos offering Caribbean Stud are taking approximately 75 cents of every dollar wagered on the jackpot and keeping it for themselves (they put the other 25 cents into the jackpot pool). Some casinos are actually keeping more, and a few (extremely few) are keeping less. No matter how you look at it, the bet is a waste of money and should be excluded from your strategic thinking. It is similar to the progressive slot jackpots—a waste of money.

How many times do the various poker hands come up in five cards? How many are non-qualifying hands?

There are 2,598,960 different poker hands that can be made with five cards. Here's how often each type will occur:

Hand	Occurrence
Royal Flush	4
Straight Flush	36
Four-of-a-kind	624
Full House	3,744
Flush	5,108
Straight	10,200
Three-of-a-kind	54,912
Two Pair	123,552
One Pair	1,098,240
Ace-King	167,280
Non-Qualifying Hands	1,135,260

What percentage of the time does the dealer qualify?

Based on the above list, we can see that the dealer will qualify 56.32 percent of the time. With this overall statistic in mind, you can see why it is fruitless to stay in any hand that is less than an Ace-King in the hopes that the dealer will not qualify. You will lose 56.32 percent of all those hands where you do so, and remember that each loss is a loss of three bets—your *ante* and your double-sized *bet* wager. If the casino did not pay out bonuses for some of the *bet* hands, it would have a staggering edge over the players. As it is, if you call the dealer by staying in on bad hands, you are asking to lose approximately an additional one-fourth of your *ante* bet in the long run. Staying in on bad hands in the hopes that the dealer wouldn't qualify was the most common mistake made by players that I talked to, and accounted for the severity of their overall losses. You can't bluff the math of this particular game by staying in on bad hands the way you can bluff a flesh and blood player at regular poker.

Based on the dealer upcard, what is the possibility of the dealer qualifying a hand?

The fact that a dealer will qualify more times with certain upcards (Aces and Kings) and fewer times with other upcards does not change our basic strategy in any way. The Five-Star Bold Card Play strategy remains the same for every dealer upcard.

Dealer Upcard	Qualifying Percentage
2	54.32%
3	54.39%
4	54.49%
5	54.59%
6	54.59%
7	54.59%
8	54.59%
9	54.59%
10	54.49%
Jack	54.39%
Queen	54.29%
King	66.43%
Ace	66.43%

Wouldn't the casino win more if the dealer-qualifying rule were not in effect? After all, when the dealer doesn't qualify he has to pay off all those ante bets. It appears this rule is actually hurting the casinos.

This is a common belief and a common mistake, for appearances are deceiving in this case. In reality, the dealer-qualifying rule is protecting the casino and hurting the player. It is this rule that gives the casino its advantage over the players, an advantage that would be approximately 18 percent were the bonus payouts not given on the *bet* wager. With those bonuses (and Bold Card Play strategy), the casino only (only!) has a 5.3 percent edge. But it is the dealer-qualifying rule that sets the stage for our defeats because it alters the math of the game so that the player loses more hands or is not paid enough on the hands that he does win. The player will lose his money in the long run because of it. If the dealer didn't have to qualify and the casino didn't give bonuses, the game would be a fair game between casino and player and, in the long run, no one would win. (With one reservation: no one would win between casino and player if the player had a big enough bankroll to handle the ups and downs of Dame Fortune.) Now, if the casinos did give the bonuses as well...well then the players would own the casinos in short order!

I never call the dealer unless I have a high pair, say nines or better, because what good is a pair of deuces?

Any pair—even those lowly deuces—is a better *bet* wager than folding. If we take a pair of deuces against any dealer upcard, we will win more (or lose less) in the long run by calling than we will by folding. If we wait to have a high pair, we'll be giving the casino a greater than *7 percent* edge over us. For example, if you have a pair of deuces with garbage against a dealer's ten, you will lose the whole *ante* if you fold your hand. But you'll only lose approximately 97 percent of the *ante* if you stay in and play it. Although it might seem ridiculous to talk in these terms, proper strategy not only informs you how to play winning hands but attempts to cut losses, however marginally, on losing hands as well. Sadly some hands are losers, no matter what you do, but what you do will affect how much you'll lose on those hands in the long run. Do the right thing and you'll lose less; do the wrong thing and you'll lose more. So call the dealer on all your pairs, even the puny deuces.

How many hands per hour does the average Caribbean Stud player play?

This is a difficult question to answer accurately because so many factors have to be taken into consideration: the speed of the dealer, how fast the players make their decisions in terms of folding or calling, and how many players are actually playing at the table. The casinos rate players based on 25 to 60 hands per hour at Caribbean Stud, depending on how many people are at a table. In chapter 8, I'll talk about comps and ratings for Caribbean Stud, Let It Ride and Three Card Poker. But this piece of advice should be engraved on your heart: the slower the pace at Caribbean Stud, the better the pace for the player; while the faster the pace, the better the pace for the casino. Speed enlivens the casinos; speed kills the players.

If I see the cards of the other players, is it possible to beat the game by using card-counting methods like the ones devised in blackjack?

Yes. It is theoretically possible to beat Caribbean Stud if you can see the cards of the other players and if you can make your decisions of calling and folding accordingly. That's why the casinos have a rule that you can't show your cards to anyone. In a paper titled "An Analysis of Caribbean Stud Poker," by Dr. Peter Griffin and Dr. John Gwynn (both professors at California State University), that was presented at the Ninth International Conference on Gambling and Risk Taking, the professors showed that the player could gain a theoretical edge of approximately 2.3 percent if he or she could see all the cards of the other players. They estimated seven players at a table in their analysis. This was better than the best edge most card counters at blackjack can theoretically get.

That's the good news.

Here's the bad news. As interesting as all this sounds, there is no *practical* way to play your hand even with this information because your brain would have to instantly compute the dealer's probabilities for making a better hand based on the information you had gleaned from those other players. The sheer number of calculations you would have to perform to come up with this information is staggering. Computers can do this but unfortunately people can't (maybe Dustin Hoffman's character, Raymond Babbit, in *Rainman* could do it as well). It goes without saying that the casinos aren't about to let you see the other players' cards anyway and they are certainly not going to pass out computers with their chips when you buy in at the game. Players must put their cards face down after they've seen them. The casino personnel strictly enforce this rule and will call a given round "dead" if they suspect certain players are trying to see the other players' cards. In fact, most casinos won't even allow a player to play two hands at the same time for fear that the information in the first hand might help him play the second hand a little better. While it's always fascinating to read about how a certain desirable thing can be accomplished, often the accomplishment of that thing is impossible in the real world. The house rules, coupled with the enormity of the counting system's requirements, negates the practical application of card counting at Caribbean Stud.

How often will I win against the dealer's hand or when the dealer folds and I call? How often will the dealer beat me?

Assuming utilization of the Bold Card Play strategy, you can expect to beat the dealer's hand approximately 16 percent of the time and lose to the dealer's hand approximately 14 percent of the time. You will call the dealer and win when he folds approximately 23 percent of the time and you will fold approximately 47 percent of the time. Looked at it this way, you lose 61 percent of the time and you win 39 percent of the time at Caribbean Stud. However, in the 16 percent of the time that you beat the dealer's hand, some of these will be for bonus wins that might keep you in the game or give you a nice win. According to the players I spoke to and the research I've done those bonus hands are what make for an interesting game,

What is the best aspect of Caribbean Stud? What is the worst aspect?

The best aspect of Caribbean Stud is the fact that you get to make choices and those choices do affect your chances. Make the wrong betting and folding decisions, play the jackpot bet, and you will be hammered by huge casino edges. Play the Bold Card Play strategy and you cut the casino edge to the minimum. So your choices do affect the outcome...somewhat. You also get to dream a little and at times, on bonus hands, some of your dreams will come true. Those are the good aspects as I see them.

The worst aspect is the fact that you are only *reducing your losses* when you make the right strategic choices. At 5.3 percent, the casino edge makes Caribbean Stud a very difficult game to beat, on any given night much less over the long run. To make a game really competitive between the player and the casino, my experience has shown that a house edge of 1.5 percent or lower is the way to go. With an edge in that 1.5 percent area, you can have many winning visits and your bankroll will tend to last a lot longer. On that score Caribbean Stud falls way short. In a comparison with another table game, roulette, that comes in with a 5.26 percent edge for the casino (just about the same as Caribbean Stud), Caribbean Stud also comes up short for additional reasons. In roulette, certain techniques can be utilized to attempt to overcome the high house edge. These include—but aren't limited to—finding biased wheels, analyzing possible dealer signatures, and visually tracking the spin of the wheel. In my view, therefore, roulette would be a superior game to Caribbean Stud if you utilize the methods I discuss in my book *Spin Roulette Gold*. For a comparison of Caribbean Stud with other popular games, see chapter 7.

What happens if there's a tie for one of the jackpot hands?

As far as I know this has never come up in the real world as the possibility of two people getting a straight flush or a royal flush on the same round are astronomical. I guess if the game continues to be played, sooner or later the event might happen. Each casino would have to handle it in its own individual way. Some might split the jackpots evenly and some might decide to give the person sitting closest to the dealer's left the lion's share. For example, if you won 10 percent of the jackpot and you were the first player, you would get the full 10 percent. The next player would get 10 percent of what remained after you got your 10 percent. On a $100,000 jackpot, you would receive $10,000 but your fellow player would receive only $9,000 as he got just 10 percent of $90,000. If a casino really wanted to be cheap, it could split the jackpot in half ($50,000 and $50,000) and give each of you just 10 percent of the half or $5,000 each. If I owned a casino I would give each player 10 percent of the total so that you and your fellow player received $10,000 each. The same problem could arise with the royal flush—do you give the first player the full 100 percent and the heck with the second player? Or do you split the jackpot 50-50? Or do you give each the entire jackpot? It would be fun to see (but, perhaps, not to experience) what the first casino to confront this problem will do. Any bets on what it will be? I predict that the casino will choose the option that costs the casino the least amount of money.

I really want to go into the math of Caribbean Stud. Can you recommend a book?

There are only two booklets that really go into the math and the numbers and have the requisite graphs and charts that a math aficionado such as you might enjoy. Some differ slightly (very slightly) in their analysis but each is a worthwhile read. You will not pick up any new strategy ideas or methods of play from them because the Five-Star Bold Card Play strategy—by any other name—is still the only practical strategy for the play of the hands at Caribbean Stud and this is essentially the strategy recommended by all the authors, with only slight variations that are not of any real consequence. However, the two treatments of Caribbean Stud do make for interesting reading for those of you who are into charts, graphs, formulas and equations. They are:

Mastering the Game of Caribbean Stud Poker (booklet) by Stanley Ko. Gambology Press, P.O. Box 82225, Las Vegas, NV 89180 ($7.95)

This is a well-written, thorough analysis of Caribbean Stud. If charts and "what if" questions are your passion this booklet supplies those in abundance. Ko has done a mammoth job of research and computer simulations to come to the conclusion that Caribbean Stud is a tough—rather, impossible—game to beat. The best analysis of the game to this point.

Expert Strategy for Caribbean Stud Poker (booklet) by Ira D. Frome and Elliot A. Frome. Compu-Flyers, 5025 S. Eastern (16), Las Vegas, NV 89119 ($5.95)

Read the above description of Ko's book and it fits the Frome brothers (their father is Lenny Frome, the dean of video poker analysts) to a tee. Although Ko has some tiny quibbles with the Fromes' recommendations, theirs was the very first comprehensive analysis of Caribbean Stud at a time when the game had just stepped off the boat and invaded Las Vegas. Not as comprehensive as Ko's book but worth a read for all the charts.

Two general gambling books and one software program also offer good information on Caribbean Stud. These are:

The Experts' Guide to Casino Games: Successful Players Offer Their Winning Formulas edited by Walter Thomason. Carol Publishing. Available from Paone Press, Box 610, Lynbrook, NY 11563 ($16.95).

This is an excellent book about most of the casino games, including sports handicapping, written by the top writers in the gaming field (okay, okay, yes, I'm a contributor as is the beautiful A.P.). The chapter on Let It Ride and Caribbean Stud is written by one of gaming's best-known writers, Henry Tamburin, and is worth a read.

Smart Casino Gambling by Olaf Vancura, Ph.D. Index Publishing Group, Inc., 3368 Governor Drive, Suite 273, San Diego, CA 92122 ($24.95)

This is a comprehensive book on several popular casino games and their mathematical underpinnings. The section on Caribbean Stud deals with the same information that both Ko and the Fromes handle but in much less depth.

Caribbean Stud Poker by Lenny Frome. Compu-Flyers, 5025 S. Eastern (16), Las Vegas, NV 89119 ($25.95)

This is an interesting and well-done interactive software tutorial for the game of Caribbean Stud. You will learn nothing new in the way of strategies but you will get to practice your Bold Card Play techniques without having real money at stake. Requires Windows 3.1 or higher. Runs on Windows 95. Available on CD ROM.

4
Bold Card Play Strategy for Let It Ride

Of the three new games that are catching on, Let It Ride seems to have the most enthusiastic following across this great, gambling nation of ours and you will find Let It Ride games almost everywhere there are casinos—it has become that popular.

With Bold Card Play strategy the player can reduce the house edge to approximately 2.8 percent, which makes it a more promising bet on the surface than does Caribbean Stud. That lower house edge probably accounts for part of its popularity.

Players that I spoke with (I interviewed 182 Let It Ride players) told me that they felt that they won more on Let It Ride than on any of the other new games they had tried. Interestingly enough, just about every player I spoke to expressed the opinion that blackjack (a game where you definitely *can* win more) was just too hard to learn to play properly and that is why they had gravitated to the Let It Ride tables. Quite a few of the Let It Ride players had formerly played Caribbean Stud but had abandoned it in favor of their new love. If Lady Luck can be fickle, then so can her acolytes.

The Rules of the Game

Like Caribbean Stud, Let It Ride is played on a blackjack-like table that can seat up to seven players. It is also played with a single

deck of 52 cards that is usually shuffled by machine, which, not sur-
prisingly, is the Shuffle-Master machine made by the same company
that developed the game (see chapter 9). As in Caribbean Stud, the
players are not allowed to exchange information about their hands
and doing so will result in a dead hand. However, unlike Caribbean
Stud, Let It Ride is not a contest of player against the dealer and there
are no messy, frustrating dealer-qualification rules to annoy you. Nor
is it like regular poker where you are playing against other players.
Instead, just like video poker, you are simply trying to get the best
possible poker hand on five cards (your three and the two community cards) to qualify for the payouts. It's that simple and this simplicity of design has also contributed to its popularity.

To play Let It Ride, you'll need three times the amount of your
bet or, at least, three times the table minimum because each round
requires three initial bets. Thankfully, as play progresses you will
have the option of removing two of the three bets, which, as I'll discuss, is the key option in the game. Without this option, the casino
would hammer all players in short order and the game would not
have caught on, since anyone who played it would now be broke,
and I wouldn't be writing this book.

Figure Two: Let It Ride Layout

In front of each player are three betting squares labeled "1," "2" and, no, not "3" but, "$."

The object of the game is to make the best poker hand that is a pair of tens or better with your three cards and the two community cards. You are not playing to beat the dealer, as I've stated, merely to get a good hand that pays a bonus according to a set payoff schedule.

Interestingly enough, unlike Caribbean Stud, this bonus schedule applies to all hands. If, at the end of play, you have three bets working, you will receive the bonus on all three bets. If you only have one bet working, you will only receive the bonus on that one bet. This feature is the psychological lure and the emotional trap for unwary players who, anxious to get the big payoffs on all three hands, will stay on hands that they should have folded.

Once the players have placed their bets, the dealer deals each player three cards and puts two cards face down as "community" cards. The players now look at their three-card hands without showing their cards to any of the other players.

The players can now decide to withdraw their number "1" bet or let it ride. To let a bet ride, a player must put his three cards face down under his wager or behind his number "1" bet. To withdraw the number "1" bet, the player must scratch the felt to indicate to the dealer that the bet is to be returned. (Blackjack players in hand-held games will recognize this "scratching of the felt" motion as asking for a hit.) Players are not allowed to touch their chips once they are on the layout so the players cannot take back their bets themselves. The dealer will push the bet back if the player so indicates.

Once the players have decided what to do with bet number "1" and the dealer has returned all withdrawals from play, the dealer now turns over the first of the two community cards. Again the players can now decide whether to take off their number "2" bet or to let that bet ride.

An important point to note is that the player who allows his number "1" bet to ride is not compelled to let his number "2" bet ride. Each bet is handled separately and there is a distinct Bold Card Play strategy for each round of play. Sadly, the "$" bet cannot be taken down (ironically, the "$" symbol really means that this is the bet where the *casino* makes its money!).

Finally, the dealer turns over the second community card and the players are paid off according to the payoff schedule, or their losing bets are collected as the case may be. Some casinos have begun to offer a jackpot for an additional side bet, as is done with Caribbean Stud. I'll discuss this jackpot bet, which comes in two varieties, one called "The Tournament" and one recently redubbed and restructured as the "Bonus Jackpot." You place this bet at the beginning of the round and it is not returnable, as are bets numbers "1" and "2."

The Payoff Schdedule for Let It Ride

Hand	Payoff
Pair of Tens	1 to 1
Pair of Jacks	1 to 1
Pair of Queens	1 to 1
Pair of Kings	1 to 1
Pair of Aces	1 to 1
Two Pair	2 to 1
Three-of-a-kind	3 to 1
Straight	5 to 1
Flush	8 to 1
Full House	11 to 1
Four-of-a-kind	50 to 1
Straight Flush	200 to 1
Royal Flush	1,000 to 1

The preceding schedule is fairly representative of the schedules across the country. However, there is a second schedule that only pays 500 to 1 on the royal flush. Obviously, given a choice of casinos, choose the one with the highest payout schedule.

As with Caribbean Stud, a word of caution concerning the payout schedule is necessary with Let It Ride. Many casinos limit the total amount that they will pay out on a winning wager. Thus, if a player betting $25 per spot were to let it ride and get the royal flush, his payout should be $75,000. But some casinos have $10,000, $25,000 and $50,000 limits. A few have higher limits. It's silly—no, let me make that stronger—it's downright *stupid* to make a bet that the house won't pay off fully if you win because of an artificial maximum payout barrier. So before you wager, multiply your three wagers by a thousand and see what you should get should luck strike and you hit the royal flush. If the payout on your intended bet is covered, then go ahead and bet it, but if your payout exceeds the table limit then scale down your wagering accordingly.

Best Strategy for Let It Ride

The basic strategy for Let It Ride is clear and relatively easy to remember.

Wager Number "1"

Before the dealer turns over the first community card, you will let your three-card hand ride if:

1. You have a pair of tens.
2. You have a pair of Jacks.
3. You have a pair of Queens.
4. You have a pair of Kings.
5. You have a pair of Aces.
6. You have three-of-a-kind.
7. You have any three cards to the royal flush.
8. You have three cards in sequence to an open-ended straight flush. (For example, 3 diamond, 4 diamond, 5 diamond can be completed with a 2 diamond and a 6 diamond or a 6 diamond and a 7 diamond.)
9. You have three cards to a straight flush with an inside draw with no card more than one spot away and with one of the following cards contained: 10, Jack, Queen, King, Ace. (For example, you have 7 spade, 8 spade, 10 spade. The 10 spade is only one card or "spot" away from the 8 spade. You could get a 9 spade and Jack spade to complete the straight flush or a 9 spade and 6 spade to do so.)

10. You will fold all other hands, including pairs that are less than a pair of tens.

Wager Number "2"

When you see the first community card, you will let bet number "2" ride if:

1. The first community card has improved any of your straight flushes from hand number "1."
2. You have paired a ten, Jack, Queen, King or Ace.
3. You have three-of-a-kind.
4. You have four-of-a-kind.
5. You have two pairs.
6. You have four cards to a flush.
7. You have a four-card open-ended straight.
8. If you have four high cards.
9. Otherwise, you will fold all hands including pairs that are less than a pair of tens.

Even with the proper Bold Card Play strategy that I have outlined, the casino will have an approximately 2.8 percent overall edge on you. If you don't use the Bold Card Play strategies, you will face much, much bigger edges.

Let It Ride: The Tournament

There are two variations that have been introduced to Let It Ride to capture the slot-playing and/or progressive jackpot lovers. The first is called Let It Ride: The Tournament. (As I write this, The Tournament is being phased out and only exists in a few isolated locations, however, this information is still valid and would, in general, apply to any bonus feature that requires an additional side bet.) For an extra dollar wager, you become eligible for extra bonus payoffs on any hand that is a straight or better. The bonus schedule is as follows:

Hand	Tournament Bonus
Straight	$20
Flush	$50
Full House	$75
Four-of-a-kind	$200
Straight Flush	$2,000
Royal Flush	$20,000

However, any players who receive a straight flush or a royal flush will be invited to participate in the tournament that will be held in a casino designated by Shuffle-Master. The tournament will consist of four rounds and all players *entering* round one will receive $1,000 as a bonus for showing up. In the tournament, the players will play with "funny money" also called nonredeemable chips. After round one the hundred players with the most "funny money" will move to round two in addition to receiving another $1,000 for advancing.

Unfortunately, or fortunately as the case may be, all players begin round two with the same amount of "funny money" once again. When round two is concluded, the twenty-five players with the most "funny money" receive another $1,000 bonus and the right to advance to round three. Round three is structured the same way as the previous two—but this time only six players will be winning the right to move to round four—the finals—but no one receives a $1,000 bonus. Why? Because everyone in the finals is a winner as the following tournament payout schedule shows:

Finish	Payout
Sixth Place	$25,000
Fifth Place	$50,000
Fourth Place	$75,000
Third Place	$100,000
Second Place	$200,000
First Place	$1,000,000

The tournament is run four times a year in various locations.

Let It Ride: Bonus Jackpot

Since many players can't take time out from their busy schedules to travel to play the tournament version of Let It Ride, Shuffle-Master has decided to create another version of the game that has a bonus jackpot similar to Caribbean Stud, although the jackpot is based on fixed schedule and is not progressive, as the Caribbean Stud jackpot is. The new bonus jackpots vary from state to state and even from location to location.

The state of New Jersey has approved the following schedule for its casinos:

HandBonus	Bonus
Three-of-a-kind	$5
Straight	$25
Flush	$50
Full House	$200
Four-of-a-kind	$400
Straight Flush	$2500
Royal Flush	$25,000

Thus, a $5 player with $15 riding on all three bets, with the $1 side bet could stand to win a total of $40,000 if he gets a royal flush (1000-to-one payout with $15 in bets = $15,000, plus $25,000 for the royal on the bonus = $40,000).

However, there are almost a score of variations throughout the country, depending on the jurisdiction. Ms. Patricia Marvel, the advertising manager of Shuffle Master, the developer of the game, was patient enough to answer all my questions concerning the bonus option. She stated: "Some pay tables start paying as low as a high pair (tens or better). Some pay tables start paying at two pair, and others at three of a kind. The top bonus payouts for the royal flush vary from $10,000 to $20,000 to $25,000. Other variations occur within the middle payouts. Some bonus pay tables pay $100 for a full house; others pay $75; still others pay $200."

The house edge on the bonus wager is determined by the looseness or tightness of the pay table. Generous pay tables that start with high pairs and give the bigger bonuses on the middle and higher hands can, according to Marvel, have house edges as low as 4.89 percent (not excessive for a side bet these days). However, tight pay tables that start with three of a kind (or higher) and skimp in the middle and top off at $10,000 on the royal flush, can have house edges that soar to 54.11 percent, according to Marvel.

If you have the opportunity to shop around (assuming you are actually interested in making the bonus side bet that is), then look for the casinos that are generous and turn your back on those that aren't.

Let It Ride Video Poker

As with Caribbean Stud, a video poker version of Let It Ride has been introduced to the casinos in an attempt to capitalize on the phenomenal success of the table-game version. The rules are exactly the same and the player can wager up to five coins just like most standard video poker games. However, to be eligible for the bonus jackpot, the player does not have to bet full coin as in regular video poker, the player merely has to place the bonus side bet. The strategy for the video-game version is the same as the Bold Card Play strategy for the table-game version.

The payout schedule for Let It Ride Video Poker is also stated in terms of "for" as opposed to "to" as was the video poker version of Caribbean Stud. Keep in mind that when you see "for" instead of "to," the payoff includes the return of your original coin. This makes the machine version of the game have a 96.4 percent return rate—a somewhat worse return than the table game.

The house has approximately a 13.5 percent edge on the bonus bet, making this feature another bad bet. The table-game version is better than the video version for several reasons, not the least of which is the comparative superiority of the payouts. Another major drawback to the video-game version of Let It Ride is that many more hands can be played than in the table-game version. A player betting $5 (five coins) can find himself playing 200 to 300 hands an hour on the machine, whereas his table-game counterpart will play anywhere from 40 to 60 hands. Obviously, it is a far, far better thing for you to avoid the video game in favor of the tables.

Payout Schedule for Video Let It Ride

Hand	Payout
Pair of Tens	2 for 1
Pair of Jacks	2 for 1
Pair of Queens	2 for 1
Pair of Kings	2 for 1
Pair of Aces	2 for 1
Two Pair	3 for 1
Three-of-a-kind	4 for 1
Straight	6 for 1
Flush	9 for 1
Full House	12 for 1
Four-of-a-kind	50 for 1
Straight Flush	200 for 1
Royal Flush	1,000 for 1
$1.00 Sidebet Bonus Jackpot	
Hand	Bonus
Two Pair	$2
Three-of-a-kind	$5
Straight	$20
Flush	$50
Full House	$100
Four-of-a-kind	$500
Straight Flush	$5,000
Royal Flush	$100,000

QUESTIONS AND ANSWERS

What are the chances that I can qualify for the tournament if and when they start up again?

Not good. The odds of getting a qualifying hand—which is any straight flush—are one in 72,193 in five cards. Those are pretty long odds. Translate that into hands played at a pace of 50 hands an hour and it will take you over 1,400 hours of play to get into the tournament. At four hours per day of play, it would take you an average of 361 days of casino play to get a straight flush. Of course, you could hit a straight flush on your very first hand and you could also not hit a straight flush until Armageddon. Considering the grinding effect of the casino's edge on the three regular bets at the game—at a rate of 2.8 percent of the total money wagered—and then the fact that that extra dollar rarely returns anything more than unrealized hopes—and you could literally be tens of thousands of dollars in the hole before you ever make it to the tournament.

In his excellent booklet, *Mastering the Game of Let It Ride*, Stanley Ko estimates that the player betting $3.00 per round on the qualifying round (which is when you go to a casino to play) will actually lose between $37,820 and $58,046 before he or she can get into the tournament. Everyone has as good a shot as anyone else to win it, which is something like 199 to 1 (sorry to dash your hopes). If you can finish in the top four, you could recoup all of your losses. Of course, almost no Let It Ride games are coming in at $3.00 minimums except, perhaps, in obscure locations around the country. Most Let It Ride games are for $5 or, just as likely, $10 minimums. Going for the gusto at these rates, can leave you tapped out.

What would be the best way to play the tournament if I got into it?

The answer to this question is merely of academic importance, as I think the best way to approach Let It Ride is to avoid the side bet that would give you a crack at the tournament in the first place. Here's a thought to turn your hair gray, or make it fall out if it's already gray, or if it has already fallen out—forget it. I don't know why I started that analogy. Instead, here's a thought to strike your heart with fear. What if you did get a straight flush, and you were invited to the tournament but business or life conspired to keep you from going? What a waste of good luck! Ko recommends playing with a team but any team, no matter how big, could get clobbered just as any player can. And any team has to divide both wins and losses among them (and they'll be more losses in this type of negative expectation game).

Now, I'll answer the question.

When you are in a tournament (and this goes for any tournament) you have to play to win—that means you should not fear busting out and losing all your funny money. That also means that you will have to judge the other players' chip stacks and not let anyone really get too far ahead. Some casino tournament players play every decision as if it's the last decision of the game.

In a tournament, you must maximize your win potential even if this takes away from your overall expectation. Tournaments are explosive contests that don't last very long. Normal casino wagering is usually a much longer, more cautious, more deliberate process (or, at least, it should be). The short duration of a tournament necessitates daring over deliberation every time.

In the Let It Ride tournament, you dare the fates by betting any hand that can give you a potential straight or flush from the get go. You bet any pair, even two deuces, because there is a chance of getting a full house. You bet any high cards in the hope of getting a pair of tens or better. In Let It Ride tournaments you really must let it all hang out and let a lot ride to have a chance to win.

Just as I wrote this, I heard from Jay Meilstrup of Shuffle Master, who told me that the tournament version of Let It Ride is definitely being phased out in favor of the bonus version. By the time you are reading this, there might be no tournament version at all. So why leave this in? Because the advice concerning tournament play is still valid for just about any type of tournament you might play in. Also, it is quite possible that tournaments might start up in the future, either in Let It Ride or in other new games. The tournament structure would be quite similar to those I described earlier. Since there's no harm in leaving the tournament information in this book, I'll do so. It can't hurt, it can only help. Good advice will stand the test of time.

How often will I win a hand at Let It Ride?

You will win approximately 24 percent of your hands at Let It Ride. Of course, in that 24 percent will be some bonus hands, occasionally some big bonus hands. Lenny Frome, in his excellent booklet, *Expert Strategy for Let it Ride,* cites the following statistics: Approximately 7 percent of your number "1" bets will ride. You'll win over 93 percent of these.

Translated into money, that means for every dollar bet, you will get back $2.40 on the number "1" bet. Not bad. On bet number "2," you will let it ride about 16 percent of the time with 90 percent of these being winners. Frome estimates that the return here is also $2.40 for every dollar bet on number "2." Again, not bad. If these two bets were all there were to the game, the players in short order would bankrupt the casinos, or own them.

The "$" bet is the opposite of what the symbol implies, as it is the party pooper that only wins approximately 24 percent of the time with a return of 60 cents for every dollar we wager (we lose 40 cents, therefore), according to Frome. Keep in mind that the "$" wager cannot be taken down and it is the effects of this poor wager that dilute the glorious expectations of number "1" and number "2" and give the casino its edge. (There'll be no bankrupting or owning of any casinos folks.)

Stanley Ko also does a similar statistical analysis but from a somewhat different perspective. His charts show that we have an almost 99 percent win rate when we have three units (bets) riding, although we will only have these bets riding approximately 7 percent of the time if we use Bold Card Play strategy. We will have two bets riding approximately 8.5 percent of the time with a win rate of approximately 86 percent. We will have only one unit in play a staggering 84.5 percent of the time but our win rate will be a dismal 11.5 percent. Ko does not break down the bets into number "1" or "2" as Frome did, but merely talks of them in the aggregate.

Both theorists paint the same picture, albeit with different brush strokes. The game favors the players heavily on the numbers "1" and "2" bets, but this cannot make up for the abysmal expectations on the "$" bet.

How often can I expect to get the various hands?

The figures following are based on five card hands.

Losing hands: 10 per 13 hands
Pair of Tens or Better: 1 per 6 hands
Two Pair: 1 per 21 hands
Three-of-a-kind: 1 per 47 hands
Straight: 1 per 255 hands
Flush: 1 per 508 hands
Full House: 1 per 694 hands
Four-of-a-kind: 1 per 4,165 hands
Straight Flush: 1 per 72,193 hands
Royal Flush: 1 per 649,740 hands

If we translate this into hours spent playing based on a fast speed of 60 hands per hour (one hand per minute), we will get a losing hand approximately 46 times every hour; a winning pair of tens or better 10 times per hour; two pairs approximately 3 times every hour; a three-of-a kind approximately once every hour; a straight approximately once every 4 hours, 15 minutes; a flush once every 8 hours, 30 minutes; a full house once every 11 hours, 15 minutes; four-of-a-kind once every 69 hours, 30 minutes; a straight flush once every 1,203 hours, a royal flush approximately once every 10,829 hours. If you played four hours a day, it would take you approximately 7 years and 5 months of playing *every single day* to hit a royal flush. The above figures are simply average approximations and if you added them up they would come out to more than 60, as I rounded to make things make sense. As I stated, you could hit a royal on your first hand, or you could never hit it. Such is the nature of chance.

If the win rate at Let It Ride is so low why do people bother to play it?

Despite the fact that you only win approximately one-fourth of your hands, when you do let your bets ride (according to Bold Card Play strategy) you are going to win more than 90 percent of those particular hands. What players find thrilling is the fact that they can be on a losing streak and then come roaring back with just a few bonus wins. It is very much like the slots, where you lose many more decisions than you win but when you do win you tend to hit for bigger amounts. Naturally, the standard fluctuations exist in Let It Ride as in all games of chance. Your bankroll will go up and down, up and down, but the real movement over any *extended* period of playing time will be down, owing to the fact that this is a negative expectation game. With Bold Card Play strategy you are reducing the house edge to the very minimum and giving yourself the best shot at taking home some money.

Let It Ride does seem to create great excitement in players. Inveterate Let It Ride players were quite enthusiastic about their experiences playing the game. Unlike Caribbean Stud players, who universally expressed frustration at the dealer-qualifying rule, Let It Ride aficionados had no such frustrations. The people I interviewed almost universally loved the game.

Susan Spector, the coauthor with gaming expert Stanford Wong of the delightful and insightful *The Complete Idiot's Guide to Gambling Like a Pro* (Alpha Books), had this to say about her first experiences with the game:

> Not only did I absolutely *love* playing the game, I may have found an exciting alternative to my mindless slot play, low-budget blackjack, and hard-driving video poker! On two occasions, after losing almost my entire session bankroll, I miraculously brought myself back and left with more than I started with. In both cases I hit a flush and in one session I got a straight. The large payouts definitely make the game worth playing—and worth sticking around for when luck seems to have taken a temporary siesta. Unlike blackjack, you don't need to bet big to win big—or to get your money back.

I believe Ms. Spector has definitely ascertained why the game is gaining so many adherents. The fact that it is possible to come back quickly with a few big hands even when you were down for an extended period is a definite plus for the players. It's a definite plus for the casinos too, as many players will hang in the game much longer than they would have normally hung in there had they been playing a different game, such as blackjack or baccarat, because they hope that the next hand or the hand after that or the hand after that will hold their comeback. Often those hands won't hold anything but more losses and the casino will collect its money.

I believe Ms. Spector also understands why people will be lured into placing the "tournament" or "bonus jackpot" side bet. She writes:

> Although I didn't put my extra dollar up because it's not optimal strategy, I may in the future because in a few short hours I gave up about a $150 worth of bonus payouts, and I'd hate to miss playing in the tournament and collecting a $20,000 royal flush payout!

Hope can be a very wonderful and a very dangerous thing and Let It Ride is certainly a game of hope.

I have stayed away from playing Let It Ride because I don't want to risk three bets at once. On a limited gambling bankroll isn't that a little risky?

In chapter 6 I will explore money-management ideas for the various games in this book. Suffice it to say that although you are indeed putting up three bets in the beginning, these bets are not writ in stone since two of them can be taken down, and will indeed be taken down the overwhelming majority of the time. The actual times when you do have three bets riding according to Bold Card Play strategy will see you winning over 90 percent of the hands—which makes these additional units well worth wagering. The problem with Let It Ride is not the extra money on bets number "1" and number "2," but rather the awful expectation of bet "$," which is where the players actually do the bulk of the losing. As far as gambling on a limited bankroll goes—welcome to the club. Unless a person is a high roller of megaton proportions, all casino gamblers are operating with limited budgets.

However, as long as your budget is sufficient for the needs of Let It Ride, then I think you can play the game.

Can I lower the casino's edge in Let It Ride if I can see the other players' cards?

If you can catch a glimpse of other players' cards you can change some of your decisions and these changes would indeed lower the edge of the casino over you. For example, if you had a 3 diamond, 4 diamond, and a 5 diamond on the first three cards and noted that your neighbor to the left had a 2 diamond, and your neighbor to the right had a 6 diamond, you would instantly know that you were not going to make a straight flush. Instead of letting bet number "1" ride, you would withdraw it.

Stanley Ko, in his booklet *Mastering the Game of Let It Ride* (Gambology Press), has a detailed strategy chart showing what to do when you can see the other players' cards. Unfortunately, this is more of an academic exercise as casino pits enforce the rule that no player can look at another player's hand. Still, as in the example above, if you do catch a peek and it is obvious that the cards in your neighbors' hands make it impossible for you to make your hand, then use the information and vary the Bold Card Play strategy accordingly.

In blackjack a player can tip the dealer by making a bet in front of your own bet for him or her. If the bet wins, the dealer wins and if the winning hand is a blackjack, the dealer is even paid three to two. Can you tip the same way at Let It Ride?

Most casinos will allow you to place a bet for the dealers on the "$" line. While a nice gesture on the part of the player, the bet's return, as we have seen, is awful. You would be much better off (actually the *dealer* would be much better off) if you gave the tip directly to the dealer. The casino doesn't want you to place bets on number "1" or number "2," as these win so frequently and for such large sums that allowing a player to bypass the "$" and bet directly on "1" and "2" would be all the motivation a dealer and player would need to form a team to beat the casinos. Imagine how much a player-dealer team could make when they won 90 percent of the time and placed the table maximum bet each and every time? Wow!

Recommended Reading

Like Caribbean Stud, there is not much out there concerning Let It Ride. However, what is out there is quite good. Here are three sources for further reading that I highly recommend.

Mastering the Game of Let It Ride (booklet) by Stanley Ko. Gambology Press, P.O. Box 82225, Las Vegas, NV 89180 ($7.95)

If charts and graphs and computer simulations are your thing, this is the booklet for you. Ko goes into tremendous detail on all aspects of the game, including imaginative discussions of "what if" situations. Reading this booklet will not increase your chances of winning over Bold Card Play but it is an enjoyable excursion into theory.

Expert Strategy for Let It Ride (booklet) by Lenny Frome. Compu-Flyers, 5025 S. Eastern Ave. (16), Las Vegas, NV 89119 ($4.95)

Lenny Frome is the dean of video poker analysts and he did the initial game analysis of Let It Ride for the casinos in Nevada. This booklet is a part of that analysis. As such, it tells you the mathematical facts that underpin the game—which are the same facts that made the casinos interested in offering the games. Frome does not use computer simulations in his booklets. He relies on mathematical formulas.

The Experts' Guide to Casino Games: Successful Players Offer Their Winning Formulas edited by Walter Thomason. Carol Publishing. Available from Paone Press, Box 610, Lynbrook, NY 11563 ($16.95)

This is an excellent book about most of the casino games, including sports handicapping, written by the top writers in the gaming field (okay, okay, yes, once again, I'm a contributor, as is the beautiful A.P.). The chapter on Let It Ride and Caribbean Stud is written by one of gaming's best-known writers, Henry Tamburin, and is worth a read.

5

Bold Card Play Strategy for Three Card Poker

Three Card Poker is a new game that is gaining a following every bit as loyal as Let It Ride. In fact, Three Card Poker seems to have the right ingredients to go the distance in the new table-game wars and surpass both Let It Ride and Caribbean Stud in popularity. The game is fast (the casinos like that); it has several different pay scales on three different hands with many bonus payments (the players like that); and the house edge on the bets doesn't exceed 2.32 percent on the worst of the three bets (gaming writers like that). The players' choices once again affect the overall expectation, but the Bold Card Play strategy is the simplest of the three games discussed in this book—and simplicity is something many casino players who are afraid of venturing to the table games want.

Created, developed, and distributed by gentleman and professional poker player, Derek J. Webb of England, it is a derivative of the card games called Brag and Flush, which were quite popular in Great Britain and India. The American version was once labeled Brit-Brag or Casino Brag before the name was changed to the easier-to-conceptualize Three Card Poker. (Doesn't the name "Brit-Brag" sound like an denture adhesive?)

The Objective of the Game

Like Caribbean Stud, the objective of Three Card Poker is to beat the dealer's hand, in this case a three-card hand as opposed to a five-card hand. There is also an added incentive in attempting to win bonuses for certain premium hands. Thus, there is competition between the dealer and the players (as in blackjack). Yet some hands win, regardless of the outcome of the dealer/player competition, like Let It Ride and slots. Three Card Poker has combined the best elements of Let It Ride and Caribbean Stud, which is another reason for its burgeoning popularity.

Procedures

Three Card Poker is quite simple to understand and play. The player can bet on three propositions called *Ante*, *Play*, and the independent *Pair Plus*. We call the *Pair Plus* wager "independent" because you can bet on it without betting on either the *Ante* or *Play*. It is very much like a slot machine in that regard. You make the bet and await the decision, which, once made, is based on a fixed schedule of payouts. You do not have to beat the dealer on the *Pair Plus* wager. If the player has a *Pair Plus*, which is any two-of-a-kind or better, he or she receives an additional payout. Many of these payouts are greater than 1 to 1. For example, three-of-a-kind pays 4 to 1 and a straight flush pays 5 to 1. The *Ante* and *Play* bets are part of the "competition mode" between dealer and player. Thus, Three Card Poker has overtones of both blackjack, where the player faces off against the dealer, and noncompetitive games such as Let It Ride, video poker and slots, where the player does not face off against the dealer. The player has the choice to play "competition" or "non-competition" or both.

The game begins with the dealer giving each player three cards and himself three cards. If you have opted to place an *Ante* bet, when you look at your three cards you must decide whether to stay in the game or fold. To stay, you must place a bet equal to your *Ante* bet in the *Play* diamond, which means, literally, that you are playing.

Figure Three: Three Card Poker Layout

To fold, you put your cards face down towards the dealer who will then collect them. When you fold you lose your *Ante* bet. Once all the players have made their decisions of whether to stay or fold, the dealer turns over his three cards. If you beat the dealer's three-card hand, you win the *Ante* and the *Play* bets at even money, which means that you win one dollar for every one dollar you wagered.

However, the *Ante* wager pays a bonus for certain premium hands such as a straight flush (usually 40 to 1), three of a kind (usually 30 to 1), a straight (usually six to one) and a flush (usually four to 1). The *Ante* also pays even money for a pair. It is important to note that although both the *Play* and *Ante* bets can be lost to a superior dealer hand, the bonus payment for premium hands is still paid even on a losing bet. This is one of the rare times in casino gaming where the player can win even when he loses!

Dealer Qualifying

Three Card Poker also has a dealer qualifying rule, just as Caribbean Stud does. What qualifies a dealer? Simply, if the dealer does not have at least a queen high or better hand, the players win on their *Ante* bets and get their *Play* bets returned. Bonus awards are not affected by the dealer qualifying rule.

Ante Bonus Payout Schedule

Hand	Ante Bonus Payout
Straight Flush	5 to 1
Three of a Kind	4 to 1
Straight	1 to 1
Flush	0
Pair	0
High Card	0

Winning Ante wagers are paid 1 to 1.
Winning Play wagers are paid 1 to 1.

Pair Plus Bonus Payout Schedule

Hand	Pair Plus Payout
Straight Flush	40 to 1
Three of a Kind	30 to 1
Straight	6 to 1
Flush	4 to 1
Pair	1 to 1
All other hands	Player loses

Best Strategy for Three Card Poker

Like all card games that require choices by the players, how you play your hands at Three Card Poker will determine the extent of the casino's edge over you. The optimum strategy for Three Card Poker when determining whether to place a *Play* bet or give up the *Ante* is— believe it or not—to *mimic* the dealer. Therefore if you have a Queen or better, place the *Play* bet. If you don't, fold your hand. Any variation from this strategy will increase (sometimes markedly) the house edge over you. I'll repeat: the best strategy for Three Card Poker is to place the *Play* bet whenever you have a hand that is a Queen or better. Any hand that is not Queen or better, fold. Simple, straightforward and, as you shall see, it is decidedly the best strategy for the game.

The house has a somewhat moderate edge on Three Card Poker when you use the Bold Card Play strategy. The *Ante* and *Play* hands face a 2.14 percent house edge, while the *Pair Plus* bet comes in at 2.32 percent for the house. The *Pair Plus* wager has no playing strategy attached to it as it operates just like a slot machine: bet your money, cross your fingers, and pray.

A conservative strategy would call for making only the *Ante* and *Play* wagers until one had a comfortable win before making several exploratory *Pair Plus* bets. If luck kept shining on you when you did so, then you would continue to play all three propositions. For truly small bankrolls, you could play the *Pair Plus* without placing the *Ante* or *Play* wagers and extend your playing time at the table without extending your risk.

QUESTIONS AND ANSWERS

What percentage of hands will a player win? What percentage of hands will the dealer win?

    Chart one shows all the possible outcomes of 1,000,000 hands of Three Card Poker if you are using the correct Bold Card Play strategy, which is to mimic the dealer and fold on any hand that is not a Queen or better. In the parenthesis, I have translated the wins into money, assuming a bet of $1.00 for each hand (*Ante* and *Play*) and, as you read down the chart, I have kept a running tally of where the player stands and the totals if the game *did not* pay out any bonus awards. Finally, I have shown how the house edge is arrived at. Chart two shows the effect of adding the bonus hands to the game. The first two charts deal with the "competition" part of the game, that is, the *Ante* and *Play* bets. Chart three deals with the *Pair Plus*, the independent, noncompetitive hand.

CHART ONE:
Competition Hands Statistics

Player folds 312,326 times.	Player loses one *Ante* bet per fold for $312,326.	Player is down $312,326.
Dealer folds 213,750 times.	Player wins one *Ante* bet per dealer fold for $213,750.	Player is down $98,576.*
Player beats dealer 210,818 times.	Player wins two bets, *Ante* and *Play* for $421,636.	Player is ahead $323,060.
Dealer beats player 206,053 times.	Player loses two bets, *Ante* and *Play* for $412,106.	Player is down $89,046.
Dealer and Player tie 57,053 times		No money won or lost

*Please note that on some hands, such as a dealer folding, the *total wager* for the player is *two times* the amount shown as a win. The money returned on *Play* is also included when figuring a total wager.

Totals:

Ties: 57,053 (two bets = $114,106)

Dealer wins 518,379 times (or 51.83 percent of total hands or 55 percent of all decisions excepting ties).

Player wins 424,568 times (or 42.46 percent of total hands or 45 percent of all decisions excepting ties).

Player loses $89,046 at one dollar per hand in 1,000,000 decisions with $1,687,674 in total wagers.

House edge without bonus hands is 5.28 percent or 5.3 percent rounded off.

In one million hands, there will be 37,105 that will receive bonus payments as follows (which means 3.7 percent of all *Ante* hands win some kind of bonus):

CHART TWO:
Effects of Bonus Hands on Player Wins and Losses

Hand	Occurrence	Odds	Total Win
Straight Flush	2,172	$5 to $1	$10,860
Three-of-a-kind	2,353	$4 to $1	$9,412
Straight	32,580	$1 to $1	$32,580

Total wins for bonus hands: $52,852

The player lost $89,046 in the "competition" but added $52,852 by virtue of certain bonus hands. The player's total loss is $36,194. Therefore the house edge on the *Ante* and *Play* wagers with bonus hands is 2.14 percent. ($1,687,674 in total wagers divided into $36,194 lost = 2.14 percent.)

CHART THREE:

Bonus Occurrence in One Million Hands of Pair Plus

Hand	Occurrence	Odds	Total Win	*Total Payout
Straight Flush	2,172	$40 to $1	$86,880	$89,052
Three-of-a-kind	2,353	$30 to $1	$70,590	$72,943
Straight	32,580	$6 to $1	$195,480	$228,060
Flush	49,594	$4 to $1	$198,376	$247,970
Pair	169,416	$1 to $1	$169,416	$338,832

* Total payout includes the return of the original bet.

Total Winning Hands: 256,115
Total Win: $720,742
Total Payouts: $976,857
Total Losing Hands: 743,885
Total Loss: $743,885

House edge: 2.32 percent

Winning-hands percentage for player: 25.61%

Losing-hands percentage for player: 74.39%

What makes Three Card Poker so popular?

Three Card Poker offers enough winning hands (45 percent) in the "competition" and a good opportunity to win bonuses on other hands (3.7 percent) that players don't feel as if they are being taken for a ride. Rudi Schiffer, publisher of *Cigars and More* and an aficionado of Three Card Poker states:

It's a really fun game that I find goes back and forth quite a bit. I enjoy it more than blackjack because of the bonus payouts. One out of four times you will win the *Pair Plus* so you never feel as if you're that far away from a win or that far away from coming back from a loss. Of all the new games introduced into the casinos in recent years, I think this is my favorite.

In your book, Best Blackjack, *you wrote that mimicking the dealer was one of the worst possible ways to play. How come it's a good way in Three Card Poker?*

In blackjack mimicking the dealer is suicide, as the house will have a 5.6 percent edge on you. As I note in chapter 7, blackjack for a basic strategy player comes in with approximately a .5 or less edge in the casino's favor. In Three Card Poker it's much different. The following list will show you the casino edge (without bonus payments) when using strategies other than the Bold Card Play strategy of mimicking the dealer. You'll note that some of them give the house enormous edges. The first strategy is the Bold Card Play strategy (without bonus), followed in descending order by the other types of strategies that might be employed by unwary players.

Strategy	House Edge
Play Queen or better	5.3 %
Play Jack or better	5.7 %
Play Queen-Jack or better	6.0 %
Play King or better	6.5 %
Play King-Eight or better	8.2 %
Play Ace or better	14.6%

It's obvious from this list that the Bold Card Play strategy is the only way to go in Three Card Poker.

What is the average hand at Three Card Poker?

The average hand, according to Prime Table Games, the company that invented Three Card Poker, is K-10-2.

What other books are there for Three Card Poker?

I'm sure that other gaming writers are analyzing and investigating the game independently, but as I write this there are no other books or sections of books—that I know of—that deal with Three Card Poker.

6

Money Management and the Mental Edge

Any time you play a negative expectation game, there is a tendency by some players to throw up their hands and say: "I can't beat this game!" Preparatory to doing this suicidal mental somersault: "Since I can't beat this game, I am therefore free to play wildly and bet like a maniac. Hell, I'm gonna lose anyway!" Believe me, this is exactly the kind of tortured logic that many players use to justify playing like idiots in games where the casino has the edge.

Listen to some voices of defeat. Peter C. of Califonria, a Let It Ride buff, states:

> I go to the casino to have fun, and I don't expect to win anything. I play until I'm too tired to focus and then I go out drinking and come back and play some more. The casinos can't be beaten. When you know that, you can have a good time and you don't feel bad about losing. Who cares about losing when you're having fun?

Estelle W. of New York put it this way:

> I'm a history teacher and I know that history teaches us that you can't win these games. I play Caribbean Stud because it's fun but I know I can't win. I play my own strategy, which is to go in on

every hand and also go for the progressive. I like the action. Since you can't beat the game why figure out the right strategy—you're just going to lose anyway? I have won a little and lost a lot but that's just the way it is. I don't even have a set strategy. I just go with my intuition.

Finally, here's Joe from Philadelphia, who was holding court in the men's room at Showboat in Atlantic City:

I don't even know why I come here [referring to the casino, not the bathroom]. I never win. You can't win. Nobody can win. I play everything, man. I piss away my money, just like this. I should stay in here all day so I don't lose my money out there. I come with five hundred bucks, man, and it don't last more than a couple of hours, no matter what I play. Nah, I've never read a book, what are they gonna tell me, how to lose my money better?

While no amount of discussion can probably convince the above three that it is better to learn the proper strategies for the games they intend to play than to throw their arms up in defeat and blithely accept their losses, the fact is that even when facing casino edges such as those in Caribbean Stud, Let It Ride and Three Card Poker, the players are not defenseless and don't have to be knocked senseless when they battle the casinos. There are better and worse strategies a player can employ as I have shown in the preceding chapters. Employ the Bold Card Play strategies and you cut the house edge; don't employ them and you cut your throat.

Good strategies are like good medicine, they delay or slow down the inevitable. It's no secret that we are all going to die (nothing like upbeat analogies to make a reader's day!), but good medicine allows us to enjoy a longer life. The first time you had a cold, or flu, or pneumonia, you didn't throw up your hands and say: "Dr. Kevorkian, come and get me!" No, you fought to stay in the game of life. Of course, we all know how the "life-game" inevitably ends—it's a negative expectation game with us on the short end—but we still keep fighting and we do indeed gain a victory here and there over death's minions every time we feed a cold and starve a fever (or is that visa versa?). Certainly, no Bold Card Play strategy can overturn the house edge in these new games because they have been mathematically structured in such a way so as to thwart any strategy that attempts to defeat them. In this, the casinos have learned a valuable lesson from blackjack—that game was introduced before anyone knew that skillful players could figure out a way to win at it in the long run.

Good strategies will *delay* the exhaustion of your bankroll in negative expectation games and position you to take advantage of luck when and if it comes your way. Still good strategies are not enough, just as good medicines are not enough, in and of themselves, to guarantee the best shot at winning. It's one thing to say that you're taking medicine for high cholesterol, but it's another to say it while you're having your fifth portion of eggs with cheese and bacon with buttered toast, slurping all of this down with a milkshake. Good medicine often has to be coupled with good life-style changes to have the best effect in life. So too, good strategies must be coupled with proper money management techniques to give you a healthy chance to stay alive in gaming.

In many ways, money management is the least understood, least appreciated, least enjoyed aspect of casino gaming. It often dictates that we leave games before we are emotionally ready to do so. It often tells us to bet less than we really want to. It often says the equivalent of: "Don't eat those eggs, here's a nice fruit platter!" Many times I will talk to people who will endeavor to play the right strategies for various games but completely scoff at the idea of managing their money properly.

Arnold J. from Mississippi said: "Heck, I come here to gamble and that's what I'm here for." Then he split his tens against the dealer's nine in blackjack—a no no.

Still, those of you who have read numerous books on gambling have probably run across several otherwise astute writers who mock the whole concept of money management. In my book, *Guerrilla Gambling: How to Beat the Casinos at Their Own Games*, I wrote what I consider to be my credo on money management. If you haven't read the book, the following will tell you exactly where I stand on the issue of money management and why I think it is almost as important as playing the right strategies. If you have read *Guerrilla Gambling*, it can't hurt to reacquaint yourself with this section.

Money Management: Sacred Cow or Silly Goose?

Excerpted from *Guerrilla Gambling: How to Beat the Casinos at Their Own Games!* (Bonus Books)

Some gamblers claim that the most important aspect of their game is money management. Others, mostly mathematicians or gaming writers steeped in math and secure jobs outside of the gambling arena, claim that money management is an illusion since most gamblers are essentially playing negative expectancy games—that is, games where the casinos have the long-term advantage. No matter how you manage your money, you are destined to go broke—sooner or later. It's just a matter of time.

I agree with the gamblers.

I agree with the gamblers because I know that the mathematicians are correct. In most negative expectancy games, sooner or later you will go broke. However, the longer you can hang in there ...the better chance you have of hitting hot streaks. So you need economic endurance.

This is the reverse of the mathematicians argument that the best way to play a negative expectation game is to take all the money that you intend to bet and bet it on one spin of roulette (on an "even" money bet) or one hand of baccarat. Go for the big one right away and, if you win, never play again. If you lose, walk away with your head held high, secure in the knowledge that you did the mathematically right thing.

Yeah, right.

Mathematicians are quite practical and have a true grasp of human nature.

Wrong.

The one guy who played like that—all or nothing on one decision at a negative expectation game—was the infamous "suitcase" player who bet almost a million dollars on the Don't Pass line at Binions in downtown Las Vegas. He had carried the money into Binions in a tattered suitcase. He put it all on the Don't Pass line. For one decision only. The first year he did this, he won. He walked out of the casino, his head held high, indicating he would never return. But, being human, he did return—the following year. Again with the tattered suitcase. Again, he bet the Don't Pass line for one decision. This time the seven was rolled on the come-out and the gentleman lost his almost-million dollars. Once again, he walked out of the casino, his head held high, vowing to never return. This time he kept his vow. He blew that high-held head of his off its shoulders with a shotgun when he got back to his hotel room. He didn't even leave a tip for the maid.

Unfortunately, real life and real gamblers are not mathematical formulas....

[This] *is my theory of money management.*

You want to be able to hang in there for as long as possible, losing as little as possible, with as healthy a bankroll as possible, so that when luck comes your way, you have the opportunity to take advantage of it and get ahead. To do this you must have enough money to weather all the inevitable cold streaks....

Money management is also character management. You have to know when to quit—when ahead or behind. The best example I can give of this just happened to me yesterday. [Obviously, the example happened many yesterdays ago now.]

I decided to take a short breather before starting this new chapter. So the lovely A.P. [my wife] *and I headed for Atlantic City for three days—Monday, Tuesday, and Wednesday. Today is Wednesday. I am not in Atlantic City, I'm home. Because I lost all my money and had to hurry home? No. I'm home because I had a single extraordinary night at the craps tables at Showboat on Tuesday; a night that saw me have my greatest roll—a 35 minute monster where I made nine points and constantly hit my numbers. It was a dream evening. A.P. estimated I hit close to 30 of my numbers, including my point, all totalled!*

On Wednesday morning (that is, this morning), the lovely A.P. looked over at me as we were eating our breakfast. I was gazing out of the window of our room—at a beautiful view of the ocean. The towering Taj Mahal was on our right. I could see the people, like ants, walking on the boardwalk, even though it was only 9 AM. In an hour or so, I would be on that boardwalk, going from casino to casino, looking for opportunities to hit and run....

"Let's pull a Captain," said A.P.

"What?"

"Let's pull a Captain," repeated A.P.

[Please note: the Captain is the world's greatest craps player. His theories form the basis for all the playing strategies found in *Beat the Craps Out of the Casinos: How to Play Craps and Win!*, *Guerrilla Gambling*, *The Captain's Craps Revolution!* and my audio cassette *Sharpshooter Craps!* Extensive interviews with him have appeared in my magazine, *Chance and Circumstance*.]

I realized what A.P. was referring to. Yesterday, the Captain and one of his Crew, Jimmy P., had been playing at Resorts where they offer 5X odds at their $25 minimum tables. If you can afford it you can take $125 in odds behind your Pass and Come bets ($150 on the five and nine). This is chump change to these two. The Captain and Jimmy were both playing the Supersystem. The first two rollers had good rolls. The Captain and Jimmy were up what for me would be a small fortune. Jimmy turned to the Captain, who was already placing his chips on the table to be colored up, and said: "Let's go home." Then they both colored up.

The four of us, the Captain, Jimmy, A.P. and I, had dinner at Capriccio, a wonderful gourmet restaurant at Resorts, and then the Captain and Jimmy headed home. They had driven one hour and 45 minutes to play for 25 minutes! They ate and went home. Of course, the Captain would be coming back in a day or two, since he plays several times a week.

"If I win early and significantly, I leave," said the Captain. "I don't give the casinos an opportunity to get their money back—on the same day! Of course, you could always say that if I stayed I might have won more. I don't buy that. I'd rather have a bird in the hand than two in the bush."

So at breakfast, the eagle-eyed A.P. was looking at me. She knew what I was thinking.

"You wanted to take a break from writing and you know that the second you enter the house, you'll be up in the office pecking away at the word processor. You're a little boy and you don't want to leave the game. But you're a little boy who has made a lot of money."

"You're right," I said.

"Let's savor the win."

She was right, of course. Savoring a win is like savoring a fine wine.

"Let's pull a Captain," I said.

We checked out right after breakfast and even as my fingers are typing this, I'm still savoring the win! It's a delicious sensation.

There was a time in my gambling career when I would not have been able to cancel a day of a casino trip because I enjoyed playing as much as I enjoyed winning. Today, I enjoy winning and playing is what I have to do to win! I believe that my character has improved with my skills over the years.

Essentially what I have just said is: "Don't play with scared money. Have enough money to back you. Know when to quit." I wanted to put this standard advice into more human terms.

How much money do you really need to play the games?

There's no easy formula for deciding such a question because we are all different. I prefer to have a lot of money backing me because I'm essentially chicken. The thought of losing my whole stake is so unnerving to me that I have built up my stake over the years to the point where I'd have to suddenly go berserk in order to put a big dent into it, much less lose it.

Some players are far more adventurous and daring. If you are the devil-may-care-to-hell-with-money (and-the-rent) type, you can probably reduce by 50 percent the bankroll requirements for playing the various games.... This reduction will mean that your chances of going broke are much greater. Your temperament must be the key to your money management decisions. You must play within your bankroll and within yourself.

I have a favorite saying: "I always gamble with one foot pointed towards the door."

Money Management for the New Games

I wish I could write that you have nothing to fear when playing the new games because my super-duper-money-management systems are guaranteed to let you come home a winner—just add water and wait for the cash to grow! Well, wishes don't always come true. I can't write those words because the new games discussed in this book are indeed house-friendly games. They might be more or less fun to play for the players, they might offer exciting opportunities to make some money now and again, but in the long run, the player is up against the wall.

My money management advice is offered in the hopes that I can cushion that wall for players interested in playing these games. I operate under the assumption that unlike the "suitcase" man of Las Vegas lore, anyone enterprising and intelligent enough to read a book on gambling is not interested in a once in a lifetime, do-or-die visit to casinoland. Instead, my guess is that most of you reading this book are recreational casino players who have found the new games to your liking or, not having played them yet, you find them intriguing. You enjoy casinos and you would like to go as often as time and your purse permit. With those thoughts in mind I have structured my money-management advice for the three new games in this book.

The House Edge and the Relativity of Time

The reason mathematicians offer the "put-it-all-on-one-bet" advice in negative-expectation games has to do with how the house edge works over time to grind down even the biggest bankrolls. Still, the mathematical number that we equate with the house edge does not tell the whole story. Caribbean Stud comes in at 5.3 percent for the house, but will that 5.3 percent translate into the same economic loss for the player as the 5.26 percent (almost 5.3) of roulette?

No. And here's why:

If we consider two games that have the same exact house edge—the game that is faster, that has the greater number of decisions per hour, will win more money for the casino and lose more money for the player in the long run, than the game that is slower and has fewer decisions per hour.

Thus, if we estimate roulette coming in at 30 decisions per hour at a crowded table and Caribbean Stud coming in at 40 decisions per hour at a crowded table, the roulette player betting $10 a spin will put $300 into action in an hour with an expected loss of $15.78 (5.26% X $300), while the Caribbean Stud player, on the other hand, will put $400 into action with an expected loss of $21.20 (5.3% X $400). That's a big difference.

Keep in mind then—whenever you read about games and per-centages and the house edge and the like—that the speed of the game is an extremely important variable and must be taken into consideration whenever we flirt with placing a series of wagers.

Here's another example:

If you were to bet a straight up Keno ticket, the house has approximately a 25 percent edge—a staggering edge in terms of math but a not-so-staggering edge in terms of actual money wagered and lost.

At six decisions per hour at Keno, the Keno player betting $10 a ticket will put a mere $60 into action with an expected loss of $15. Even with the huge house edge, a Keno player in this example fares better—economically speaking—than does a roulette player or a Caribbean Stud player. Naturally, Keno does not offer the kind of action most casino gamblers want and has never caught on as a big game. You'll see more napping than clapping in most Keno lounges.

The point remains, however, that the number of decisions must be taken into consideration along with the house edge to determine just how tough a game actually is and just how big a bankroll you really need to play it. The casinos prefer their games to be played fast, faster and even faster than that. We players, on the other hand, should look for more leisurely paces at the games where the casino has the edge and we should have enough money not to sweat out our level of action...which leads to my money-management tips.

Money-Management Tip Number One: Create a Gaming Bankroll

If you're like me, you don't relish the thought of taking your kids' college funds and blowing them at a casino. You don't even like the idea that you are gambling with money that could (or should) be used for something else. (Some senior citizens, however, might be downright gleeful to be playing with their ungrateful children's inheritance, to whom I say, "have fun and live it up!") To avoid that horrible sense of guilt associated with playing with junior's college tuition, it is a wise gambler who sets aside money specifically earmarked for playing. A separate bank account that is only tapped for gambling purposes is a nice reliever of guilt. I know this for a fact.

Whenever I used to play with money I needed, I couldn't fully enjoy myself—even when I won. The terror that I could lose money that might be needed for something else, something real, was just too much for my timid nerves. So I saved up my money over a period of time, opened a separate bank account, and then—while I still hated to lose—when I did lose I didn't feel as if I had betrayed God, kids and country because a session or two went badly. Although I would never say not to think of gambling money as "real" money, it should be thought of as real money that *cannot* be spent on "real" things such as education, food, clothing, and the like. Nestled comfortably in a bank account all its own, your gambling stake's sole purpose is to ease whatever residual terror you might feel when you place a bet in a casino. The money is indeed "real" but it is really just for gambling.

By way of analogy: I had a good friend in college. He was a bit of a worrier. One day we were at a bar drinking some beer and this other kid, an arrogant premed student, came in and ordered a coke. He then turned to my friend and said haughtily: "Even a thimbleful of beer kills dozens of brain cells and your brain cells are the only cells in your body that can't be replaced."

My friend turned pale. He had just finished a hefty mug of beer.

"Really?" he asked, now thoroughly worried. "Just a thimbleful?"

"Yes," said the other kid smugly drinking his coke. Then he emphasized: *"And...brain...cells...can't...be...replaced."*

After a few moments, my friend asked: "How many brain cells do we have?"

"Billions and billions," said the smug coke drinker.

"Billions and billions?" my friend asked.

"Billions and billions," nodded the premed student knowingly.

My friend paused, looked at me, then turned to the bartender and said: "Oh, in that case—give me a pitcher!"

The fact that he had billions of brain cells in reserve was such a comfortable feeling that he decided he could afford to have his beer and drink it too!

Having a bankroll specifically set aside for gambling purposes will allow you to say: "In that case, let's go to the casino!" the next time someone criticizes you for engaging in such an economically dangerous pursuit.

Money Management Tip Number Two: Slow Down the Game

In games where the casino has the edge, the tortoise might not win the race, but he doesn't wind up in the soup quite as fast. (Is there such a thing as tortoise soup? I know there is such a thing as turtle soup, which I had in New Orleans.) Play like a rabbit and you'll wind up in the stew quite quickly. (I *know* there's such a thing as rabbit stew!) There is absolutely no reason to play like a lightning-fast machine at any of the games in this book. Since you do have choices to make and the dealer must wait for you to make them, then take a deep breath, an even deeper thought, and a few moments of stall-time before you plunge in. If you can slow down the pace by just 10 percent, you will find that not only does your money last longer but you are getting comped just as much as if you *had* played that extra percentage of time. Another way to really cut down the amount that you are playing—but *not the amount of time* that you are playing—is to sit out a hand or two every now and then. If you were to, say, sit out one hand in five, you would be cutting your exposure to the house edge by a full 20 percent! Yet, you would still be in the casino, at the table, playing for whatever amount of time you want to play.

How important is speed for the casinos? Here is an excerpt from a press release by Shuffle Master, Inc., the designers of Let It Ride. This press release was sent to casino executives in the hopes of getting them to put the Shuffle Master automatic card-shuffling machine in their casinos. Note the importance of the number of decisions (speed of the game) in the press release:

> Shuffle Master created and developed the automatic card shuffler which has virtually revolutionized card dealing in the gaming industry. *The shufflers can produce a minimum 25% increase in hands dealt per hour, and in many cases much higher, depending upon*

the game and the normal house procedures, which translates into a sig-
nificant revenue increase for the casino. An increase in hands dealt
also means an increase in player satisfaction and enjoyment, as a
result of more hands played and a faster pace. [italics mine]

Ignoring the last sentence, which is really saying that players
like it more when they lose more, you can see that the casinos and
their products providers are well aware of the relationship of speed
to the bottom line. So should you be. Memorize the words to that
Simon and Garfunkel song that goes: "Slow down, you move too
fast/got to make the morning last...." Just substitute the word
"bankroll" for "morning" and the song is quite relevant to casino
players.

Money Management Tip Number Three: Play at Crowded Tables

Blackjack card counters love to play heads-up (one-on-one) with
the dealer because they can get more hands in. That's fine because card
counters enjoy a slight edge over the casino. We want to do the opposite at Caribbean Stud, Let It Ride and Three Card Poker. "The more
players at the table the merrier!" should be our motto. We want to dif-
fuse all those hands that can be played in a given time period over as
many players as possible. (If we could we should hang a sign at our
table that says: "WELCOME!") By the way, the casino makes just as
much money whether one player plays a total of a hundred hands or
whether four players play a combined total of a hundred hands (25
each). But if you are one of the four players playing 25 hands each, you
will lose a lot less than if you're the one player playing 100 hands!
Playing with other players can also help to slow down the game as
many table-game players are social sorts and enjoy talking and laugh-
ing. The more everyone talks and laughs, the fewer number of hands
per hour. So brush up on your social skills and head for the crowded
tables.

Money-Management Tip Number Four: Play the "Least" You Can Afford

This tip might sound strange as it is the reverse of the "only play what you can afford to play" tip that most gaming writers give. I'm telling you to play the *least* you can afford to play (as opposed to *what* you can afford to play) in order to get what you want from the game. So what do you want from the games you play? Excitement? Well, if playing the table minimum gives you plenty of excitement, play the table minimum. If not, move to the level of play that gets your heart beating, but not fibrillating, and play at that level. But no more, even if you can afford to.

Do you want comps? If having RFB (room, food and beverage) is what you're looking for (see chapter 8) then find out what the *minimum* is to achieve the level of comps you desire and only play that amount. If you have to play $100 per hand at Let It Ride to be eligible to be treated like an avatar-returned-to-save-the-earth at the casino of your choice, then don't you dare bet $101 per hand!

Excitement, comps, whatever, play the *lowest* level to get the level of excitement and/or comps you need, but not one penny more. And play that *lowest* level at the *slowest* possible pace!

Dollars and Sense

Although the number of decisions per hour will differ from table to table (A lot of happy talkers? Slower pace. Sullen, angry gamblers? Much faster pace.) and from dealer to dealer, the following money-management scheme is based on my research into how casinos judge the speed of the various games for the purposes of comping. Most players will put in three to five hours of play on a given day when they visit a casino. The formula I have set up for determining what your session stake should be is based on the number of decisions-per-one hour of play with a playing session lasting no more than two hours. Such a gaming bankroll for a given session will almost assure that any cold streaks won't devastate you. Later in this chapter I'll talk about what to do on the hot streaks.

The Formula for the New Games

The formula for establishing a session bankroll (or session stake) for the new games is based on the following answers to the following logical questions:

A. How often do I intend to visit a casino?
B. How long will I play when I'm there?
C. What level of play interests me?

You must decide how many visits you are going to make, but, when in doubt, always estimate high. So if you think you're going to a casino two or three times a month, figure three times. Again you must determine how many hours you're going to play. The formula is DPH x .50 (decisions per hour multiplied by one-half). If a game generates 50 decisions per playing hour, then you need 25 times your bet for an hour of play (50 X .50 = 25). If you intend to play for four hours, then you would need 100 times your average bet to play the game with almost no risk of going broke. If you intended to visit the casinos three days at that level of play, you would then need 300 times your bet (100 average bets X 3 days = 300 average bets).

However, the maximum you would need for a realistic bankroll would be 500 times your bet. At 500 times your bet, you could safely visit the casinos for many months without worrying about being wiped out. Keep in mind that all three games tend to lose you more hands than they'll win you—thus, your bankroll heads for the cellar—until you hit a bonus hand or two and come (hopefully) roaring back. And that's why you need a seemingly larger bankroll than for other games such as craps and blackjack.

Caribbean Stud

A full table of six or seven players at Caribbean Stud will see approximately 40 hands per hour played. Play alone and you can expect to see almost 100 hands per hour! Don't play at tables with fewer than four people or you're asking for trouble.

At a full table, you would need 20 times your bet to play for one hour and 40 times your bet to play for two hours. A wise player will spread out his play over several sessions in a given day. Maybe four sessions of one hour each or two sessions of two hours each. I have given you the amount you need to play at various levels for various time periods. I would not recommend playing more than four hours a day (which is usually what you need to achieve whatever comps you desire or deserve for your level of play). Eight hours of play would constitute two days at a casino. Maximum bankroll is the total amount you should have in reserve to play the game under the assumption that you intend to go to the casino at least a "few" times a year for a "few" days each.

Avg Bet	1 hr	2 hrs	3 hrs	4 hrs	5 hrs	6 hrs	7 hrs	8 hrs	Bankroll
$5	$100	$200	$300	$400	$500	$600	$700	$800	$2,500
$10	$200	$400	$600	$800	$1,000	$1,200	$1,400	$1,600	$5,000
$15	$300	$600	$900	$1,200	$1,500	$1,800	$2,100	$2,400	$7,500
$20	$400	$800	$1,200	$1,600	$2,000	$2,400	$2,800	$3,200	$10,000
$25	$500	$1,000	$1,500	$2,000	$2,500	$3,000	$3,500	$4,000	$12,500
$50	$1,000	$2,000	$3,000	$4,000	$5,000	$6,000	$7,000	$8,000	$25,000
$100	$2,000	$4,000	$6,000	$8,000	$10,000	$12,000	$14,000	$16,000	$50,000

The above chart shows that if you were going to visit a casino for two days, you would bring $800 if you intended to play a total of eight hours at five dollars per hand. The chance of losing this amount is remote. Whatever happened, win or lose, you would return home with some money, which would be put back into your gambling account.

Let It Ride

A full table of six or seven players can expect to have approximately 35 to 40 hands per hour. If we take 38 hands per hour as our average for Let It Ride, we can easily figure out what we'll need to play this game based on our formula DPH x .50. (Again you do not want to play Let It Ride all alone at the table where you can receive up to 100 hands per hour!) Since you are playing slightly fewer hands per hour in Let It Ride than in Caribbean Stud, and at a lower house edge, I have reduced the total bankroll requirement proportionally to 475 times your average bet.

Avg Bet	1 hr	2 hrs	3 hrs	4 hrs	5 hrs	6 hrs	7 hrs	8 hrs	Bankroll
$5	$95	$190	$285	$380	$475	$570	$665	$760	$2,375
$10	$190	$380	$570	$760	$950	$1,140	$1,330	$1,520	$4,750
$15	$285	$570	$855	$1,140	$1,425	$1,710	$1,995	$2,280	$7,125
$20	$380	$760	$1,140	$1,520	$1,900	$2,280	$2,660	$3,040	$9,500
$25	$475	$950	$1,425	$1,900	$2,375	$2,850	$3,325	$3,800	$11,875
$50	$950	$1,900	$2,850	$3,800	$4,750	$5,700	$6,650	$7,600	$23,750
$100	$1,900	$3,800	$5,700	$7,600	$9,500	$11,400	$13,300	$15,200	$47,500

Three Card Poker

Although Three Card Poker comes in with the lowest house edge of all the new games, it has many, many more hands per hour in terms of speed of play. Casinos estimate that at a full table, you can get anywhere from 60 to 80 hands per player per hour. Wow!

Wow, that is, if you're the casino.

Pow, that is, if you're the player.

Remember that many players will have three bets riding on a number of these hands. If they aren't following the proper Bold Card Play strategy, two of these bets will have rather hefty house edges. I think it would be a fair estimate to say that at a talkative, happy table with six or seven players, the casino would realize approximately 68 hands per hour (maybe fewer if you really talk it up and slow down the game). In addition, with Three Card Poker, we have to take into consideration the fact that one of the bets—the *Pair Plus*—is an option that not all players will take.

The first chart will show the bankroll requirements for the play of the *Ante* and *Play* hands. The second chart will show what is required if you decide to bet the *Pair Plus* as well.

Total bankroll requirement is 544 times your minimum bet (owing to the reduced house edge, the total in reserve does not have to be quite as big proportionally). You might be able to get away with less since the house edge is lower for Three Card Poker compared to Caribbean Stud and Let It Ride. However, I would follow the chart because it is quite possible that you might find yourself with dealers who deal many more total hands per hour (and players willing to go speedily along with them). If so, you'll want as much backing you as you can get.

Three Card Poker: Ante and Play Wagers Only

Avg Bet	1 hr	2 hrs	3 hrs	4 hrs	5 hrs	6 hrs	7 hrs	8 hrs	Bankroll
$5	$170	$340	$510	$680	$850	$1,020	$1,190	$1,360	$2,720
$10	$340	$680	$1,020	$1,360	$1,700	$2,040	$2,380	$2,720	$5,440
$15	$510	$1,020	$1,530	$2,040	$2,550	$3,060	$3,570	$4,080	$8,160
$20	$680	$1,360	$2,040	$2,720	$3,400	$4,080	$4,760	$5,440	$10,880
$25	$850	$1,700	$2,550	$3,400	$4,250	$5,100	$5,950	$6,800	$13,600
$50	$1,700	$3,400	$5,100	$6,800	$8,500	$10,200	$11,900	$13,600	$27,200
$100	$3,400	$6,800	$10,200	$13,600	$17,000	$20,400	$23,800	$27,200	$54,400

Three Card Poker: Ante, Play, and Pair Plus Wagers

Avg Bet	1 hr	2 hrs	3 hrs	4 hrs	5 hrs	6 hrs	7 hrs	8 hrs	Bankroll
$5	$255	$510	$765	$1,020	$1,275	$1,530	$1,785	$2,040	$4,080
$10	$510	$1,020	$1,530	$2,040	$2,550	$3,060	$3,570	$4,080	$8,160
$15	$765	$1,530	$2,295	$3,060	$3,825	$4,590	$5,335	$6,120	$12,240
$20	$1,020	$2,040	$3,060	$4,080	$5,100	$6,120	$7,140	$8,160	$16,320
$25	$1,275	$2,550	$3,825	$5,100	$6,375	$7,650	$8,925	$10,200	$20,400
$50	$2,550	$5,100	$7,650	$10,200	$12,750	$15,300	$17,850	$20,400	$40,800
$100	$5,100	$10,200	$15,300	$20,400	$25,500	$30,600	$35,700	$40,800	$81,600

Three Card Poker: Pair Plus Wager Only

Avg Bet	1 hr	2 hrs	3 hrs	4 hrs	5 hrs	6 hrs	7 hrs	8 hrs	Bankroll
$5	$85	$170	$255	$340	$425	$510	$595	$680	$1,360
$10	$170	$340	$510	$680	$850	$1,020	$1,190	$1,360	$2,720
$15	$255	$510	$765	$1,020	$1,275	$1,530	$1,785	$2,040	$4,080
$20	$340	$680	$1,020	$1,360	$1,700	$2,040	$2,380	$2,720	$5,440
$25	$425	$850	$1,275	$1,700	$2,125	$2,550	$2,975	$3,400	$6,800
$50	$850	$1,700	$2,550	$3,400	$4,250	$5,100	$5,950	$6,800	$13,600
$100	$1,700	$3,400	$5,100	$6,800	$8,500	$10,200	$11,900	$13,600	$27,200

Overview of Betting Schemes for the New Games

When I presented these figures during a lecture on bankroll at a seminar I was conducting, one member of the audience was outraged. "You mean to tell me that to play Let It Ride at $25 a hand, I have to have $12,000 in the bank? At $25 a hand, it will take forever to go through that $12,000. Your money-management advice is ridiculous!"

In some ways this fellow was right, of course. Any money management scheme that bets into a negative expectation game is "ridiculous" because in the long run it is doomed to fall prey to the house edge. However, the figures I've cited are not ridiculous if we look at a finite period of time, say, a person's gambling lifetime, which can be defined as how many days that person will spend at a casino for the rest of his or her natural-born days. Is almost $12,000 too much in reserve to play Let It Ride?

I don't think so.

Here's why:

Stanley Ko figured out the expected loss and standard deviation for any number of hands of Let It Ride ranging from 1,000 to 700,000. Given a speed of 38 hands per hour, how many days of play would we need to reach certain hand totals? The following chart shows how many hands of Let It Ride constitute a given number of hours. I have then translated the hours into days (assuming you play four hours per day) and what Ko estimates the won-lost range will be. The won-lost range is the *most* you can reasonably expect to win in a given period of time (or hands) and the *most* you can reasonably expect to lose. Obviously, most of us will fall somewhere between the extreme points. The figures are based on a 99.7 percent certainty, meaning that this scenario will occur 99.7 percent of the time. What happens the other .3 percent of time? Anything!

I have used $10 as the betting unit as this is a reasonable table minimum throughout the country for Let It Ride. (I've also rounded the figures.)

Although Ko's statistics go on up to 700,000 hands (I don't think anyone will be spending 18,420 days in casinos playing any of these three games any time soon), the following chart is enough to explain some truths. If you take a close look at these figures, you can see the devastating effects of the house edge on a $10 player. After spending 66 days in a casino (almost two days a month for almost three years—a not unreasonable number for many casino habitues), a $10 bettor could, if Lady Luck were cruel to him, lose upwards of $14,000. Even if his luck were mediocre, he could easily be down half that much.

Number of Hands	Total Hours	Total Days	Won-Lost Range
1,000	26	6.5	+$2,898 to -$3,692
5,000	132	33	+$5,384 to -$9,351
10,000	263	66	+$6,452 to -$14,387
20,000	526	132	+$6,800 to -$22,670
40,000	1,053	263	+$4,969 to -$36,708
50,000	1,316	329	+$3,461 to -$43,136

Now, if you take a look at the chart on page 84, for $10 players, you'll note that I have given $4,750 as a total bankroll for this level of play. Although the figures for total bankroll might at first appear "ridiculous," they are not in fact so. The reason I like to lay it out in this way is to graphically show you how much you really can go through in your playing of a given game—even with the best of strategies. So the $25 player with a $12,000 bankroll is not absurd—he's merely *prepared*.

What these Figures Mean for Your Bankroll

I do realize that many people who go to casinos are not about to put significant amounts of cash away for their gambling bankrolls. It's not something most people are used to doing or used to even thinking about. People often say to themselves before they go to a casino: "Hmm, I think I'll hit the bankbook for $500 for a trip to the casino." Then they take the $500 and go to the casino. If this is you, then here's what I would recommend. By all means take that $500 out of your normal account. You obviously know that you can afford to play with this money. But—this is a big *but* here—only take $250 to the casino. Take the other $250 and put it in a *new account*. There, you now have a gambling account. Simple.

When you do go to a casino, I would recommend that you at least have the necessary bankroll to last a couple of days at the desired level of play. More often than not (in fact way more often than not), you will come home with some money, although not necessarily a win. If you go to the casino with $250 and come home with $125, put the $125 in the separate account with the $250 that's already there. Now, you have $375 set aside for gaming purposes. On your next trip, go to the *regular* bank account and take what you figure you can afford to lose—say another $500—and do the same thing. Put half of it in the gaming account and take half to the casino. When you come home, hopefully with some money, or even some money over and above your initial amount (a win!), you put it all in the gaming account. In this way you can actually build up a gambling bankroll slowly and—relatively—painlessly. The times that you win, all the money should go into your gambling bankroll—the win and the initial stake. Don't spend it on other things. One or two big wins can go a long way towards creating a hefty bankroll that you can now use exclusively for gambling.

Many people have IRA, Keogh or 401(k)s and the like for retirement. Their companies (or they themselves) have a little money taken out of each paycheck, which is then put into an account that is strictly for retirement. You can do this for gaming purposes as well. Take a small percentage of your pay—say 2 percent to 5 percent per week—and put it aside. Such a small percentage will not hurt your finances (I assume)—you won't even notice it. But in time it will grow large enough to give you plenty to play with. The need for a bankroll is obvious. If every bet you place conjures up the thought that you are using Tiny Tim's operation money, you will never be able to enjoy the gaming experience.

Many players are not aware of how destructive the casino edge can be over extended periods of time. In the short run, we look at a given day of wagering as a close contest with not all that much money at stake (relatively speaking). Yet, as you can see from Stanley Ko's figures, over a reasonable period of time (10,000 hands or 66 days) you are incurring a substantial risk. The bigger your bankroll, the softer the impact of that house edge on your emotional state. Like my friend said, when informed that we had billions of brain cells,

"Bring me a pitcher!" Negative expectation games can have a negative affect on your psychology as well as on your wallet.

Another reason to have as large a bankroll as humanly possible concerns the effects of a big bankroll when matched against a little bankroll. (I cover this concept in depth in my audio cassette tape *Power of Positive Playing*.) Remember that even in a fair game, the huge bankroll beats the little bankroll almost every time. The casinos have monstrous bankrolls. Even if the new games were even contests where neither you nor the casino had the edge (which they aren't), the casino would probably beat you because your bankroll is just too small to compete over an extended period of time. The effects of math compound the effects of the casinos' large bankrolls, making it that much tougher for the player to compete. All the more reason to puff up your economic arsenal. Bold Card Play strategies have given you the best strategic weapons to contest the mighty casinos, your own husbandry and thrift must now come into play to get the financial wherewithal to engage in the games without having angina every time you have a losing session.

When to Say Adios, So Long, Goodbye, I'm Outta Here, or Sayonara to a Session

The fact that you are playing a negative expectation game—as just about all casino players are—does not mean that you *must* lose each and every time you play. If that were so, casinos would have the level of excitement of a funeral home on a slow night. In fact, the Bold Card Play strategies coupled with playing at full tables, where you slow down the pace as much as you can without drawing attention to yourself, along with the proper bankroll for the bets you intend to make, will give you an excellent shot at winning in the short run. You string enough short run wins together and you might find that you are one of the "lucky" ones who actually have a positive economic experience in the casinos. It is not impossible to win. It is just improbable. Sadly, our own emotions often betray us when the casino edge hasn't touched us.

Although I have written about the time you will play in terms of hours and days and so forth, the fact remains that at any given session at any given moment a little voice will speak to you in your head and say: "It's time to go." For the experienced and savvy player, that little voice represents an unconscious mechanism that has added up the amount of time you've played, the adrenaline rush you've had in your gambling experience, the amount you've won, or lost, or the amount you came back, or the amount you dropped from when you were at the peak of your winning. That little voice is usually right. It knows that the session is coming to an end. It knows that the time to get out is now.

I recognize that some people (even those of you have played in casinos quite a bit) might have perverse "little voices" speaking in their ears: "Tony, bet the mortgage!" "Denise, you really don't need to eat tomorrow and the kids are all fat anyway!" "Freddie, swallow the dice and a black chip before the dealer can stop you." However, I am hoping that these people aren't reading this book.

Those of you who have casino experience will probably be able to relate to this "little voice" idea of mine more readily than someone who is new to the casino experience.

Here's a little quiz you can take to ascertain whether you have the experience necessary to develop a "little voice" of your own. If you answer yes to any of the following questions, you have enough casino experience to sculpt a fully functioning "little voice."

Did you ever go back to your room and ask your spouse or significant other, or the first person you saw in the elevator, to give you a good swift kick in the thing-that-you-substituted-for-your-brain when you continued to play after you had had a significant amount of money (and felt like you should leave)?

Did you ever wish you had a sign on your back that said "kick me" when you had made an extraordinary comeback from a deep hole (and felt like you should leave) but didn't?

Did you ever ask for a severe *scolding* from the first person who reminded you of your third grade teacher, the severe Miss Cribbs, when you had lost your session stake and you had headed for the ATM when you knew you should have been heading out the door?

"Put on the BIG boots Wilma and give me a swift one where my stuffed wallet used to be!" could be sung as a refrain for almost every casino gambler sometime or other. Many of us have experienced this state of affairs—we had it and we blew it.

I recall one of my favorite episodes of one of my favorite sit-coms, *The Honeymooners*. Bus driver Ralph Kramden [Jackie Gleason] has just found a suitcase full of money—unfortunately it's all counterfeit—and being a guy who wishes to be a big shot, he goes out and spends, and spends, and spends some more. He treats people to clothing and other goods. He just gives the money away. He tips everyone for everything! Even his mother-in-law (a cantankerous old battle axe who on Ralph and Alice's wedding day said: "I'm not losing a daughter, I'm gaining a ton!" in reference to the largish Ralph) has come around to lovingly calling him: "Sonny boy!" because of all the money he's given her.

Of course, when it is discovered that Ralph has been spending "funny" money, he is once again a loser. His only defense was to snap his fingers and say: "I had it and I went with it!"

In the real world, it isn't quite as easy to snap our fingers and say, "I had it and I went with it!" because, unlike Ralph, we are not sit-com characters forever doomed to being what we don't want to be—losers. We are real people who can take the money and run!

One question that I am most often asked during a speaking engagement on money management and the mental edge is: "How do you know when to leave?" I give the "little voice" example for experienced casino players who invariably nod and understand that on countless occasions that voice spoke to us and was right, damn it! For novices, relative novices, or people who don't hear "little voices" in their head, I have to give concrete suggestions. If you are new to casino gaming or don't yet have a "little voice" that you have cultivated (or trust), I'll give you some concrete suggestions for when to say farewell to a game.

1. In all the new games, the chance to *quickly* hit it *big* exists. You could walk into a Caribbean Stud or Let It Ride game, get a straight flush, and you're in the pink, or, rather, you're in the green! Or you could hit a hot streak where you get several full

houses, threes-of-a-kind, flushes and straights. Suddenly you're up quite a bit of money in quite a little time. Yet, emotionally, you don't feel like leaving—you haven't played enough to satisfy you and you feel that you need more action. In that case, consider doing this. Continue to play but only play with half of the win. I call this the *Half and Half* money management system. Say you've hit a hot streak and you're now up $1,000. Take $500 of the win and play with that. Your initial stake and the small win are now "out of bounds" so to speak.

Next, anytime you win a hand, take half the win and put it aside as well. So, let's say you won $1,000 and you have given yourself $500 of the $1,000 to play with. You have "locked up" the $500 win and your initial session stake. You are now guaranteed that this session is a winner.

Now, you start playing with the $500. On the next hand, you win $10. You now take $5 of that win and put it aside. The other $5 goes back into your playing fund along with the original $10 bet. So you're now playing with $505 and you have $505 as a guaranteed win in your "out of bounds" pile. When you lose a bet, you lose it all. Playing this way, you will guarantee that you will leave with *more than* the win you initially set aside.

2. In games where Lady Luck is using you for a footstool, you'll want to get out when you lose your session stake. That's a given. You will never *ever* allow yourself to lose more than your session stake. ATM machines are the enemy of money management and should be avoided.

However, those of you who play more than the table minimum can consider reducing your bet after a series of losses in order to s-t-r-e-t-c-h your playing time in the hopes of hitting a big one. Even if Lady Luck continues to boot you around, you will not lose any more than that session stake but you will lose it over a *longer period of time*. However, if your luck changes, just a few good hits—even at a reduced bet—will usually be enough to bring you all the way back or close enough. Reducing a bet in a losing streak at games with bonus prizes is not a bad way to play. It gives you more time at the table, for the exact same risk.

Still, once you've come all the way back (or almost all the way back), consider this a sign that Dame Fortune had pity on you; now take her hint and take a hike.

3. After several hours of play, if you are ahead by however much, take a certain amount—say three or four bets—and say to yourself: "When this goes, I go." You might lose those three or four bets in short order and in short order you'll be heading for the cage to cash in your win. If, on the other hand, you continue to win, then keep playing—until you lose those three or four bets. Or, use the *Half and Half* formula above—take half of all wins and use those to play with and take the other half and add it to the money you aren't touching.

4. Never leave *while* you're winning. You might have won the last hand when your little voice said, "Time to go." If you are ahead and the next hand will not put you in the red, then play the next hand. If you lose *that*, then leave. If you win that, keep playing until you lose that one hand. I remember once when I was ready to go, I said, "I'll play this one hand and if I lose I'll leave." I won seven straight hands until I lost that one hand. Then I left.

   Do not do the opposite. If you are down by only one or two bets when you feel that it's time to go—don't try to get even, don't try to recoup those one or two bets. Just go. The tendency in such a close loss is to try one more hand, and if that loses, then one more hand, then one more hand after that to get yourself even. Before you know it you have a much more substantial loss and what could have been called a "push" is now a plummet. Many gamblers being one or two bets down do not feel a compulsion to be brutally honest when friends ask how they did. So these gamblers say, "I'm about even." This small untruth is a convenient way of saying, "I lost" when that loss was only a few bets. Remember that in Let It Ride and Caribbean Stud, you are going to lose many more hands than you win. If it's time to quit—one hand down or not—it's time to quit! Remember it's easier to say, "I'm about even," than to say, "I stayed too long and got my buttocks kicked but good."

Questions and Answers on Money Management

What if I am ready to go, and I say, "I'll play one hand," then I hit a winning streak; now I don't want to leave after that one hand anymore? So what do I do?

Then don't leave. Go with the *Half and Half* method. Take *half* of what you just won and play with that. When you lose *that*, leave the game. Say, you were going to leave after one hand and then, as I did, you won seven in a row. Say, you are now up, oh, $300. Take $150 and play with that. Put the other $150 in your pocket. If you should turn that $150 into $300, then take another $150 and put it away. Keep doing this until you lose the $150 or until the end of time, whichever comes first.

I happen to like this *Half and Half* formula. It assures that you will take a win from the session but it also gives you a shot at milking that win or, at the very least, extending your playing time for the purposes of comps or satisfaction. I do realize that many players need to play a certain number of hours to satisfy their urge for action and this way of handling a winning session is a good way to do that.

You always hear the term "quit while you're ahead." So when is the exact moment to do this? When you're "X" amount ahead? "Y" amount? What is the definition?

If you have played an emotionally satisfying time (you'll have to give "emotionally satisfying time" your own personal definition), and if you will go into the red if you lose the next bet, quit right then and there. A small win or a push is often all you can hope for in a given session. Take a break with the thought that your bankroll is still whole and ready to go into the next session. If you are ahead, play just one more hand—until you lose that hand as I mentioned before. Again, never leave *while* you're winning.

Would the technique called TARGET work for finding tables that are friendly to the players? I understand this is a technique used by blackjack players to find tables that favor them. What about "charting" tables as some craps authors recommend? Would this work in Let it Ride and the other card games?

The TARGET technique that you are talking about is indeed a highly controversial method of trying to find "player-biased" tables in blackjack. It is the blackjack equivalent of charting tables in craps. TARGET was created by gaming author Jerry Patterson for the blackjack shoe games, which are, according to Patterson, not shuffled properly (properly = randomly) and thus lend themselves to prolonged bias either in the dealer's or the player's favor. Most blackjack authorities dismiss the TARGET concept (some quite violently—Patterson has been called all manner of names by his fellow blackjack writers) because it is unprovable mathematically or by computer simulation. You either buy into the premise or you don't.

Some of the ingredients in TARGET: for example, you look for tables where players have plenty of chips in front of them (this shows that they've probably been winning), or where cigarette ashtrays are full (this means people have been playing a long time, which probably means they've been winning), or where people seem happy (happy people are probably winning). These methods can indeed be used to pick a table in Caribbean Stud, Let It Ride, and Three Card Poker. There is a reservation to doing this: *when in doubt, follow the math.* For example, even if two happy people are playing at a table and there are four empty seats at that table, while the table next to them has only one chair open with several less-than-happy players, go to the table that has more people, even if they aren't all that happy. You do not want to put yourself into a position of playing an enormous number of hands at a negative-expectation game. That's following the math.

TARGET and other "charting table" techniques fall into a category of playing techniques that I consider thusly: *All other things being equal, if it doesn't hurt you to follow the method, then follow it.* It is in fact much nicer coming into a game where players have been winning—it certainly feels good. So, you have two tables side by side and one has six people who are cursing, foaming, frothing, and demented-by-their-incredible-losing-streaks and the other table has six people who are counting their chips, smiling, singing songs of praise to the gods of their choice, then you'd be an idiot not to go to the empty chair at the happy, smiling, singing table. You would always play the proper Bold Card Play strategies for all the games—no matter whether the dealer was losing, not qualifying, et cetera—and you would always play based on your bankroll and the size of the bets you can afford to make. However, with that in mind, it certainly can't hurt you to look around for crowded tables with happy people. (Note: I would personally avoid the tables with the ashtrays loaded with butts because it means either the waitresses aren't clearing the tables properly or that you'll be breathing through a nicotine fog during your playing session.)

When should I increase my bet?

I realize that for some players, there is a thrill in increasing, perhaps even in parlaying bets (doubling the last bet on a win) to go for that really big win. However, the games of Caribbean Stud, Let It Ride and, to a lesser extent, Three Card Poker, have such abysmal player-winning percentages (remember that in Let It Ride you only win about one-fourth of your hands!) that escalating your bets can wipe out a win rather quickly. If you have won a bonus hand or two and you are now in the black, you could easily lose it all back by precipitously increasing your bets.

With that very strong word of caution, if you are still enchanted by the idea of increasing bets to go for the big win, then follow this advice: if you have tripled the amount of your session stake, consider increasing your bet by a third. Thus, if you have brought $1,000 to play, if you now have $3,000, and if you have been playing at the $10 level, go to $15. However, do not allow yourself to lose more than half your win (that is, $1,000) before dropping back down to $10 or, better still, calling it a session.

Sometimes you speak of sessions and sometimes you speak in terms of hours played, decisions per hour and so on. What are the differences among them?

In some ways, they are all the same thing. A session is a defined period of playing, whatever the criteria is for defining "period." Such criteria could be time as in an hour, two hours, three hours or more. It could be a given number of hands—say 68 hands, or 136 hands or more. It could be until you win or lose a set amount of money. Casinos don't talk of sessions when they discuss the merits of a game. They usually discuss a game based on decisions per hour. In Three Card Poker, with 68 decisions per hour, a player playing an hour-long session is obviously playing 68 hands. A player who has decided to play 68 hands as a session will (probably) play for one hour. Only if a session is defined as a predetermined win or loss will we see wild results. For example, what if I say that I will play until I've won $100, then on the first hand I win $500. That session will last one decision and a few seconds. Usually players that create sessions in terms of win goals and loss goals can reach those rather quickly. On the contrary, they might never reach their goal if it is stated as: "I will bet $5 per hand and I will play until I win $10,000 or lose $50,000." A player could spend an eternity (okay I'm exaggerating for effect here) attempting to have a session such as that.

When you are deciding upon your sessions, you will have to take into consideration whether comping comes into your thinking. If the casino wants you to play for a set time period to get the comps you are looking for, then you will have to give them the time (or make it appear that you are giving them the time—see chapter 8). One of the worst money-management schemes I ever heard of was the player who told me: "I play until I lose 16 hands in a row!" It is highly possible that such an occurrence might not happen for a long, long time. Imagine what you would lose on the following: you lose 8 hands in a row, win 1 hand, lose 6 in a row, win 1 hand, lose 15 in a row, win a hand and on it goes, short, medium, and long losing streaks punctuated by the occasional win. You could lose your entire bankroll in such a case.

I prefer a looser concept of session based on some correlation between time-spent, amount of money established beforehand, a win or loss. Experienced players—especially players who play tough with the casinos—usually have that "little voice" that tells them when to call it a session.

Until you develop the "little voice," use the advice in this chapter.

7

Comparison of Casino Games

Just as people come in all manner of shapes, colors and sizes, so too do casino games. Usually when we talk of house edges we talk in terms of a fixed percentage that the house takes from every bet. So if the house enjoys a 2 percent edge on a game, we can safely say that for every $100 bet at this game, in the long run the house will keep $2 Still to analyze various games for comparative purposes, it is important to realize that another ingredient is perhaps equally important—how many decisions per hour a game theoretically enjoys.

If we took a game with a 2 percent house edge and a game with a 5 percent house edge we might be able to state that we will actually *lose less* in an hour of play at a 5 percent game than we do at the 2 percent game. The number of decisions per hour is the key to making such a judgment. If the 2 percent game has 100 decisions per hour and the 5 percent game has 30 decisions per hour and we start with a $1,000 bankroll, making $25 bets at each game, we lose $50 per hour at the 2 percent game (100 decisions X $25 X .02 = $50) and only $37.50 at the game with a 5 percent edge with 30 decisions (30 X $25 X .05 = -$37.50). It would theoretically take us 20 hours to lose our entire $1,000 bankroll at the 2 percenter, while it would take almost 27 hours to lose the entire bankroll at the 5 percenter.

So, a true comparative analysis of various casino games has to take into consideration the house edge of the games *and* their number of decisions per hour.

There is, however, a third consideration that is just as important to my way of thinking. The games you choose to play must fit your temperament. Action players who need many decisions per hour to get that adrenaline rush will champ at the bit if they had to play Keno where decisions come every eight minutes or so. Then again, some people can't lose too many sessions without becoming shell-shocked. For example, individuals who want to become expert video poker players often find themselves disheartened when they play machines where the players have the mathematical edge because that "edge" is only realized when a player hits his or her share of royal flushes (a royal flush is a give-or-take 40,000 to 1 shot!). Video poker players must understand that they will lose a greater number of actual sessions than they will win but once their ship comes in their overall bankrolls will increase. A player must have the temperament to put up with all those losing streaks. If not, their ship will be the Titanic.

Blackjack is another story altogether. While losing streaks—some quite extended—are a part of the game, most expert blackjack players tend to win the majority of their sessions—even 60 to 70 percent of them—over extended periods of time. While this sounds nice (and, actually, *is* nice), the effort required to learn the basic strategy and card counting techniques (as well as other refinements to the game) are not to everyone's liking. For such people, even a long-term positive monetary expectation can't make a game that requires so much effort fun to play.

My comparison of the games is therefore based on three factors: house edge, decisions per hour, and the nature of the game. I have given what you can reasonably expect to win or lose per hour of play at the games betting a reasonable $10 per decision, but I have also explained the flow of the game. Obviously, I have had to take an educated guess—based on the statistics of the casino industry—as to how many decisions-per-hour a given game has. While I might be off in my calculations of decisions-per-hour (some casinos rate blackjack at 100 hands per hour, some at 60, while still other casinos estimate all of the numbers in-between), I am probably close to, or right on, the mark when it comes to the comparative relationship of the games. The casino advantage in games where the players actually make strategic decisions or choose between bets will show various figures—the highest figure for those playing the proper basic strategies or best bets, and the lowest figure for those playing their own strategies or worst bets (players who place the worst possible bets are considered "action players" by the casinos). If three ranges are given, the middle range comprises everything in-between the best and worst bets. The figures are composites of the various figures I have seen used by the casinos. Since there is a range for the "decisions-per-hour" based on the various casino formulas I am acquainted with, the final totals are based on an average of the high and low figures. Thus, in roulette, I will use 30 decisions per hour as my number to ascertain what you can reasonably expect to lose per hour in the long run since the range is 25 to 35 decisions per hour for that game. So it will go for all the games analyzed.

ROULETTE DOUBLE ZERO WHEEL

Casino Advantage:	Decisions per hour :	Loss Per Hour:
5.26% (inside/outside bets)	30	$15.78
4.15 % (inside/outside bettor*)		$12.45
2.63% (outside bettor only*)		$7.89

*Casino returns half of losing bet when 0 or 00 is the decision.

ROULETTE SINGLE ZERO WHEEL

Casino Advantage:	Decisions per hour :	Loss Per Hour:
2.70% (inside/outside bets)	30	$8.10
2% (inside/outside bettor*)		$6.00
1.35% (outside bettor only*)		$4.05

*Casino returns half of losing bet when 0 is the decision.

Nature of the Game: Roulette is a leisurely, low-pressure game. Inside bettors, those bettors who bet directly on the numbers, will find that they can lose almost all their bets in a given hour of play but one or two hits that pay off at 35 to 1 will bring them right back. Roulette can also offer a quick strike for large wins —if the player can quit while he or she has the money in hand, that is. Outside bettors will win almost half their decisions, so it will be a seesaw affair for extended periods of time. However, the slow grinding effect of the casino's edge will make itself evident in time. Outside bettors who play in casinos with surrender, especially those on the single zero wheel, will be able to play many hours without having to worry about being wiped out. Outside betting in roulette is conducive to extended playing sessions, inside betting to big wins and bigger losses (see my book, *Spin Roulette Gold: Secrets of the Wheel* for the complete analysis of all aspects of roulette).

CRAPS

Casino Advantage:	Decisions per hour :	Loss Per Hour:
.02% to .82% (best bets)	100	$4.20
.83% to .1.52% (typical bets)		$11.80
1.52% to 6% (action player)		$38.00

Nature of the game: The action is fast and furious with a host of bets—some excellent, some awful—to choose from. Much money can be won or lost at this game in the blink of an eye, as most players bet on multiple propositions—some excellent, some awful. It is a roller-coaster of ups and downs that requires a strong stomach (see my book, *Beat the Craps Out of the Casinos: How to Play Craps and Win!* and my audio cassette, *Sharpshooter Craps!*).

BLACKJACK

Casino Advantage:	Decisions per hour :	Loss Per Hour:
0% to -1.5 (expert player)	80	0 to (+ $12.00)
.25% to .52% (basic strategy player)		$3.12
1% to 1.5% (typical player)		$10.00
1.6% to 5% (action player)		$26.40

Nature of the Game: Excellent players at blackjack can cut the house edge to almost nothing (expert players can actually get the edge). To become an excellent player you have to learn basic strategy, which takes one to two weeks of memorizing. Excellent players will win approximately 44 percent of their hands and lose approximately 48 percent with the other 8 percent being pushes. Excellent players will win almost half their sessions but, over time, the slow grinding of the house edge will be evident on their bankrolls. Typical and "action" players will find that they lose the great majority of their sessions due to improper play. For "action players" blackjack is a frustrating experience and you'll see them pounding tables and cursing. This game is awful on the nerves if you don't know what you're doing since you make choices that come back to bite your wallet (see my book, *Best Blackjack* for more information).

BACCARAT

Casino Advantage:	Decisions per hour :	Loss Per Hour:
1.27%	60	$7.62
(typical bank/player bets only)		
2% to 10% (action player)		$36.00

Nature of the Game: Baccarat is another leisurely game that has elegance, style, a low house edge, and basically a single decision—do I bet player or bank? The third bet, TIE, is a sucker bet that very few good baccarat players make. I think I might actually be overstating the number of hands per hour because at a full table, it can take two minutes to complete a decision. One of the reasons that baccarat tables rarely have every seat taken is the fact that the house minimums are usually quite high—$25 and up—and thus it is a game that tends to favor those whom fortune has favored in matters of birth or business.

MINI-BACCARAT

Casino Advantage:	Decisions per hour :	Loss Per Hour:
1.27%	100	$12.70
(typical bank/player bets only)		
2% to 10% (action player)		$60.00

Nature of the Game: This is the fast-action version of the slower-moving baccarat. Here the dealer deals all the hands and quite a few decisions can be made in that time. If you are going to bet $25 per hand, you would be much, much better off playing the big-boy version of baccarat instead of its speedier little cousin.

PAI GOW POKER

Casino Advantage: Hour:	Decisions per hour :	Loss Per
2.5% (all players)	45	$11.25

Nature of the Game: Yawn! Slow moving, deliberate, many non-decisions per hour. It is theoretically possible to get a slight edge at this game but it is practically improbable as it requires a person to bank the entire game. The cost is prohibitive for most players. This is the casino equivalent of going to the library to read a book. You get your cards, you think about your cards, you set your cards, you see what happens. The downside is that you do have to memorize a very, very long index of strategy decisions that are harder to remember than blackjack decisions (see my book, *Guerrilla Gambling: How to Beat the Casinos at Their Own Games*).

RED DOG

Casino Advantage:	Decisions per hour :	Loss Per Hour:
3% to 6% (all players)	80	$36

Nature of the Game: This game offers some choices in terms of strategy but doesn't seem to generate the excitement of most table games. You will rarely see more than one or two people ever playing it in a casino. Maybe that's because it is associated with those games we played as a child.

SIC BO

Casino Advantage:	Decisions per hour :	Loss Per Hour:
2.8% (good player)	100	$28
8% to 30% (all other players)		$190

Nature of the Game: In almost every way, one of the worst table games ever introduced into a casino—if not the worst of all time. It combines sky-high edges on most bets with a tremendous number of decisions per hour. This game appeals to people who enjoy bunji jumping with frayed cords. The betting is similar to roulette or the Big Wheel, but even the Big Wheel, a notoriously bad casino game, looks good compared to Sic Bo.

CARIBBEAN STUD

Casino Advantage:	Decisions per hour :	Loss Per Hour:
5.3 % (bold card play)	45	$23.85
6.7% (action players)		$30.15

Nature of the Game: Players' choices do count but the game has its frustrating moments due to dealer qualifying rule. This is the single greatest detraction from the game from the player's point of view.

LET IT RIDE

Casino Advantage:	Decisions per hour :	Loss Per Hour:
2.8% (bold card play)	40	$11.20
3.8% (average players)		$15.20

Nature of the Game: This game does offer players real decisions that affect the outcome. However, this game can be frustrating, as you lose approximately 75 percent of your hands and you could go—for an hour or two—steadily into a hole. The flip side is that it can be exhilarating on the hands you win because these are often for large amounts and you just might climb out of that hole (if you're in one) or to the top of winner's mountain if you were even or close to it when the big hands came.

THE BIG WHEEL

Casino Advantage:	Decisions per hour :	Loss Per Hour:
14.8% (all players)	100	$148.00

KENO

Casino Advantage:	Decisions per hour :	Loss Per Hour:
25% (all players)	10	$25

THREE CARD POKER

Casino Advantage:	Decisions per hour :	Loss Per Hour:
2.2% (bold card play*)	70	$15.40
3.9% (action players)		$27.30

*assumes player is betting Pairs Plus option as well as Ante/Play

Nature of Game: Fast, fun, and offers some choice. The downside is that it is indeed *fast* and *fun* offers some choice but not quite enough to offset the fun-fast element that can make you lose sight of how much money you're actually wagering over time.

Hierarchy of Games Estimated Cost Per Hour

If we just take the objective areas of the above analysis—loss per hour based on my estimates—we can make a chart as to where each game stands in relation to every other. I must caution the reader at this point to realize that I am not including advanced strategies such as the Captain's *5-Count* at craps in this hierarchy, although I will include card counting. This chart is simply to put the new games into some kind of context within the table-game kingdom. Cost is *per hour* and is once again based on *$10 per decision*.

1. Blackjack - expert play: 0 to +$12.00
2. Blackjack - basic strategy: -$3.12
3. Roulette - single zero wheel, outside bets w/surrender: -$4.05
4. Craps - best bets: -$4.20
5. Roulette - single zero wheel, all bets w/surrender: -$6.00
6. Baccarat - typical player: -$7.62
7. Roulette - double zero wheel, outside bets w/surrender: -$7.89
8. Roulette - single zero wheel - all bets: -$8.10
9. Blackjack - typical player: -$10.00
10. **LET IT RIDE - BOLD CARD PLAY: -$11.20**
11. Pai Gow Poker - all players: -$11.25
12. Craps - typical bets: -$11.80
13. Roulette - double zero wheel, all bets w/surrender: -$12.25
14. Mini-baccarat - typical player: -$12.70
15. **LET IT RIDE - ACTION PLAYERS: -$15.20**
16. **THREE CARD POKER - BOLD CARD PLAY: -$15.40**
17. Roulette - double zero wheel, all bets: -$15.78
18. **CARIBBEAN STUD - BOLD CARD PLAY: -$23.85**

19. Keno - all players: -$25.00
20. Blackjack - action player: -$26.40
21. **THREE CARD POKER - ACTION PLAYERS: -$27.30**
22. Sic Bo - good player: -$28.00
23. **CARIBBEAN STUD - ACTION PLAYERS: -$30.15**
24. Baccarat - action player: -$36.00
25. Red Dog - all players: -$36.00
26. Craps - all bets: -$38.00
27. Mini-baccarat - action player: -$60.00
28. Big Wheel - all players: -$148.00
29. Sic Bo - action players: -$190.00

Obviously, the new games of Caribbean Stud, Let It Ride, and Three Card Poker are not in the top category of casino table games, but they aren't in the basement either. A $10 player playing Bold Card Play strategies is basically losing one bet an hour at Let It Ride and 1.5 bets an hour at Three Card Poker. These are averages and long run expectations. Individual sessions will vary wildly. You'll also note that the Bold Card Play strategies certainly do cut your risk compared to typical or action players. It is quite possible that as these games become even more popular certain modifications will take place that will decrease the casino edge even further as player volume compensates for house edge. A slight tinkering with the bonus schedule of payouts for all three games would go a long way to reducing the house edge and increasing player interest. Casino executives in high competition areas should give some thought to competing for Caribbean Stud, Let It Ride and Three Card Poker players as they do now for blackjack and craps players.

8

Compliments of the House

I remember hearing my next door neighbor in Brooklyn—a big, burly teamster who drove a gigantic truck—*whine* to his wife and children: "Can't I get a little consideration around here?" after someone had eaten this perfect apple that he was saving in the back of the refrigerator for that special moment at night (the otherwise quiet teenage daughter was the chief suspect of her brothers and sisters who had also found favorite foods missing from time to time). "I work like a dog and all I want is the damn apple I saved. You all know that was *my* apple and I'm entitled to it!"

When I was younger, I never understood this idea that if you work for something you are *entitled* to it and that those who are in your support should not have access to the things you are saving for yourself. They are *not entitled* to anything. I just figured the guy was infantile to be making such a big deal over a silly apple in the back of the refrigerator.

Had I known better at the time, I would have realized that to my neighbor this apple was more than *just* an apple—just as the apple that Adam and Eve ate was more than *just* an apple, but a sign that they had disrespected and disobeyed God. To my neighbor this apple symbolized his position in his household, his own Garden of Eden, and that his wishes, indeed his demands, should have been given precedence over everbody else's. Of course, we all want to be the gods of our own Gardens of Eden, and to be obeyed and respected by those we support, those who should be grateful enough to want to do our bidding. The fact that his daughter (I *know* she did it) had the temerity to disobey him and eat that apple had stripped him of his status in his own little garden. None of us want that.

Well, the world of the casino is no different than the world my neighbor lived in or the world of Adam and Eve. It is a Garden of Eden of a different sort, with an apple every bit as alluring as the apple on the Tree of the Knowledge of Good and Evil of which Adam and Eve partook, a fruit every bit as desirous as the apple in the back of a teamster's refrigerator. The apples of many casino players' eyes are called "comps." Comps (short for *complimentaries*) are the "little considerations" casino patrons get in the form of free or discounted rooms, food, drinks, shows and other services from the casinos where they risk their hard-earned money. The type of comps that a player gets determines his or her status in the hierarchy of the casino kingdom, which, in a very real way, the player is supporting.

Of course, the casinos are more than willing to give players special complementaries and privileges, just as the teamster's daughter was more than willing to eventually give Dad the respect he desired after he decided that he would pay for her wedding. She even apologized for the apple incident as she picked out her flower arrangements and hired an expensive band to play at the wedding. If you spend enough on your gaming—be it at the machines or at the tables—the casinos too, will be dutiful children and give you all the respect, all the comps, all the consideration you could ever want.

And there's the rub.

Although comps exist for just about every level of play in a casino—from handing out rolls of coins to rolling out the red carpet—many casino players have no idea of what their action is worth to the casinos in which they play. Even today, there are many players who have no idea that they can get any consideration at all.

Naturally, most casinos don't make it easy to know what the real criteria is for the various levels of comps that exist. You never see the formulas posted at the tables where we play or in casino newsletters. Most players know in a hazy, nebulous way that if they bet black chips ($100) and higher, they can get just about anything they want. They also know that if they bet at the single red-chip level ($5), they're going to have to play a long, long time to get the cost of a sandwich, or an apple. But in the great world of the in-between, in that quantum-mechanical realm of several red chips-per-bet to a few green chips-per-bet, lies the great "cloud of unknowing" concerning just what our action is worth to the casino comp counters. And this is exactly how the casinos want it to be.

In researching this chapter, I contacted many casinos' public relations departments. I had a list of specific questions that I wanted answered concerning their individual comp policies. I faxed these questions to them. I wanted to know just how hard a player had to work to get access to that apple at the back of the refrigerator. In fact, not one—*NOT ONE* casino—was willing to answer any of the questions (on the record that is) that I had concerning their particular comp policies. Most were willing to give me generic statements like: "We reward our players for their play." Thanks, but I knew that.

Similar to the Garden of Eden story where Adam and Eve have no idea of the cost of their disobedience to God prior to their meal (after all, they had no knowledge of what the threatened "death" meant—or even what "pain" was—as no evil existed in their garden), the casino player has no real understanding of just how his play is rated and what "considerations" he or she can get because of it. "We reward our players for their play" is almost as vague as saying "You're going to die" to someone who doesn't know what death is. "We reward our players for their play" doesn't really tell us anything we really need to know.

But being a dogged sort, I went to my moles in the various casino hierarchies to get the desired information. Here's what one casino executive, a good friend of mine, who wished to remain anonymous, told me:

> Frank, the reason we don't want to publish the *exact formula* for table play at the new or the old games is because some of the judgments are subjective. Once we put something on paper and distribute it to players, we're locked into it. Once you write about it, we're stuck. You can't believe the number of arguments pub-

lishing the paybacks for table game comps can cause. In slots it's easy—you can accurately monitor a machine's play, but in table games, the floor people do the rating and no one is infallible. I once worked in a casino that said they would give you back the table minimum for every hour of play in the form of comp coupons. People sat at the tables with watches! Then people argued over whether our promotion really meant table-minimum or their minimum bet. Some people would only play every other hand but still wanted a comp for an hour. I spent my time in the pit refereeing fights all day.

Another casino executive told me:

If you write that our casino will give 'X' amount in comps for a certain level of play, we'll have all sorts of problems because some people will give us 'X' action and we still won't want to comp them 'X' amount for other reasons. We want to keep the comp ball in our court and that's why we prefer to keep the information proprietary.

All casinos do have formulas, which I'll explain, but they also have certain intangibles that have to be taken into consideration that can't be expressed as a number in an equation. In his very worthwhile book, *How to Be Treated Like a High Roller Even Though You're Not One* (Carol Publishing), Robert Renneisen, the president of the Claridge in Atlantic City, writes:

Some customers come frequently, for instance, and, although on each individual visit they may not gamble enough to warrant a comp, their continued patronage should get them one from time to time just because they are regular customers....Issuing comps isn't an exact science...it's a decision.

Another Atlantic City executive stated: "Players are the lifeblood of a casino and in return for a player's patronage we are willing to return a certain percentage of their action in the form of comps. The more action a player gives us, the more comps they get."

A casino defines "action" as the total amount of money a player risks, or is willing to risk, over a given period of time. A high-action player (the highest of which are known as "whales") is one who bets a lot for a long period of time. Low-action players (sometimes referred to as "fleas" or "barnacles") will bet small over short periods of time. Big-time players get big-time comps—called RFB (for room, food, and beverage)—which will garner them free rooms or suites, free gourmet meals, free limo or helicopter rides to and from home, and even reimbursement for plane fares. They will also be invited to all the exclusive parties where they can hobnob with celebrities being paid to hobnob with them. Small time but "rated" players—defined as those who put in the requisite number of hours to qualify for comps—can get occasional free or discounted rooms (usually Sunday through Thursday), free or discounted meals (in the buffet or cafe), and free or discounted shows. They will also get invited to parties on special occasions as well, although not the big ones, and certainly not New Year's Eve. (Keep this in mind: small-stakes' players at smaller casinos that cater to their level of action will loom larger in the minds of the casino executives of those establishments.)

But how does a casino decide who gets what and for how much? Are blackjack players, craps players, roulette players, baccarat, Let It Ride, Caribbean Stud, and Three Card Poker, slot and video poker players all judged equally? How does change in a machine match up against chips on a table?

My moles in the casino industry all told me the same basic thing. All casinos use a flexible yet relatively standard formula that takes into consideration the average size of the player's bets, how long he/she plays, as well as the type of game he/she plays (games are rated based on decisions per hour as noted in chapter 7), and whether the game or the player's skill level gives the casino a high house edge or a low house edge or, in some cases, *no* house edge. Intangibles are also taken into consideration such as how often a player comes to the casino, how many friends—who play—he or she brings, and what that person's past performance has been.

Yet, not everyone can get rated. Robert Renneisen states in his book that a card counter's action at blackjack, no matter how much he bets, is worth nothing to a casino. One casino executive went even further and stated: "A card counter actually hurts us. Why should we give an individual a comp who has an edge over us? Let him buy his own sandwich." However, a typical blackjack player, one who plays his own brand of basic strategy, is giving the casino edges of one to four percent or even more. These individuals the casino will comp to high heaven—as long as they keep playing poorly.

As a savvy gambler, you must ask yourself these two questions before pursuing the world of casino comps:

1. Are the comps I'm looking for worth the risk I'm taking?
2. How much is that comp really costing me?

A blackjack card counters playing at $1,000 a hand and up can make money over time by exploiting their edge (between .5 percent and 1.5 percent depending on the types of games they are playing)—enough so that they can pay for their own RFB. But the "average" blackjack player "earns" RFB many times over by poor play.

Caribbean Stud, Let It Ride and Three Card Poker players must play the Bold Card Play strategies to keep the house edge to its minimum. Curiously enough, most casino executives that I spoke to *did not* make distinctions between Bold Card Play strategies and the awful strategies that most players employ at these new games. Instead—everyone who played the new games was given the benefit of the doubt—*they were all rated as awful players!* In fact, the casino assumed poor play as a norm (in fact, it is!) and those of us who don't play abominably are getting an added benefit in the comping realm. For example, instead of averaging 2.8 percent as the house edge for Let It Ride, many casinos were using 3.8 *or more* as a norm! Great! We good players are getting one or more percent on comps over what our action really deserves—and that ain't hay, folks. (How long this type of situation will last is anyone's guess. Casino executives are a smart and frugal bunch these days—when they read this book, they might tighten their policies. But my advice to players is to enjoy it while it lasts and, maybe, try to make it appear that you play dumb without actually doing so.) It is quite evident that the Bold Card Play strategies that I have delineated in this book, coupled with generous comps, can make for a much closer contest between player and casino than the mathematics of the new games might at first indicate. There are some tricks you can employ to get more comps than your action is truly worth. I'll explain those at the end of this chapter.

How Casinos Rate the Players

Just about every casino in America has some type of player rating system, usually with *player cards* that are given free to the players who sign up for them (these look like credit cards). They are also referred to as *comp cards* in some casinos. Sometimes just signing up for a card can bring a host of initial comps, so sign up for as many player or comp cards as you can—even if you don't intend to play much in a particular casino. Some casinos will literally give you money to sign up for their players' cards. Whenever a casino shows you the money, take it! Whenever you go to a table make sure that you hand in your card and that the floor person records your name.

That's the first step, getting a rating card (and some initial comps) and then getting rated in the casinos where you want to play. The second step is to understand what your style of play is worth to the casino.

The basic formula for table games is this: AB x HP x SG x CA = PTL x PR = CP; which in English is: (average bet) x (hours played) x (speed of game) x (casino advantage) = (player's theoretical loss) x (percentage return) = (comp points). Every casino determines for itself what figures it will plug into the formula. There is a general agreement in casinos throughout the country as to the overall hierarchy of speed concerning the games (although the range within games differs somewhat), but most casinos definitely differ on how much they will return in the form of comps. This difference in return rate is, in the words of one casino spokeswoman, "proprietary," which in English means, "We're not telling anyone so don't ask us again, Frank."

But this I can tell you. Some casinos are tight and some are loose with the comps. The casinos that tend toward high-end play, tend to be tight and the casinos that cater to low rollers tend to be loose. A $25 player at the Mirage on the Las Vegas Strip might get a buffet or, if he puts in the time, the cafe; while that same player will be treated like a high roller at the Lady Luck in downtown Las Vegas. However, all casinos tend to tighten up their comp policies on weekends and loosen them during midweek. It is easier to get comps in the off-season (Vegas in summer, Atlantic City in winter for example) and harder to get comps during the "on" season. Just try getting a comp on New Year's Eve if you're playing $10 per hand—if you can find any ten dollar tables on New Year's Eve that is!

The following chart will give a generic version of how casinos rate the various games and the players who play them. This was culled and collated from the information that my various moles hidden deep within the casino industry revealed to me. Don't be fooled by the casino jargon such as "action player" because often when casinos refer to "action players" what they really mean is "dumb players" who give the casinos a tremendous edge (see chapter 7).

How Much Can Your Play Get You In Comps?

In general, casinos are willing to give back between 30 percent and 50 percent of a player's theoretical loss in the form of comps. Remember the key words here are "theoretical loss." You don't have to *actually* lose any money to get comped. However, the casinos know that in the long run, most players lose in reality—and especially in the aggregate—what their theoretical loss profile indicates.

If we take an average of 40 percent as our return on a theoretical loss, we can now determine approximately what our play is worth to the casino by plugging some numbers into the formula: (average bet) x (hours played) x (speed of game) x (casino advantage) = (player's theoretical loss). Then we take 40 percent of the theoretical loss and that tells us how much the casino is willing to give back to us in comps. Here's another thing to keep in mind: the fact that the casinos are *willing* to offer us comps does not mean that they are *obligated* to do so. Writes Renneisen: "Comps are courtesies extended by the house—they're not part of [a player's] birthright."

For the highest level of comps casinos prefer that players put in four hours of play per twenty-four hour period. Naturally any number of

COMPLIMENTS OF THE HOUSE

hours can be plugged into the formula. However, the following comp chart is based on four hours of play at Caribbean Stud, Let It Ride and Three Card Poker. I am plugging the *casinos' percentage* into the formula for house edge and not the Bold Card Play strategies, which, as you'll see, are somewhat lower than the casinos' estimates. (Hooray! One for our side!)

CARIBBEAN STUD:

House edge: 5.3 percent; 45 decisions per hour; 4 hours of play; 40 percent return.

Betting Level	Theoretical Loss	Comp Return
$5	$47.70	$19.08
$10	$95.40	$38.16
$15	$143.10	$57.24
$25	$238.50	$95.40
$50	$477.00	$190.80
$100	$954.00	$381.60

LET IT RIDE:

House edge: 3.8 percent; 40 decisions per hour; 4 hours of play; 40 percent return.

Betting Level	Theoretical Loss	Comp Return
$5	$30.40	$12.16
$10	$60.80	$24.32
$15	$91.20	$36.48
$25	$152.00	$60.80
$50	$304.00	$121.60
$100	$608.00	$243.20

THREE CARD POKER:

House edge: 2.5 percent; 70 decisions per hour, 4 hours of play; 40 percent return.

Betting Level	Theoretical Loss	Comp Return
$5	$35.00	$14.00
$10	$70.00	$28.00
$15	$105.00	$42.00
$25	$175.00	$70.00
$50	$350.00	$140.00
$100	$700.00	$280.00

Scobe's Ten Com(p)mandments:

1. *Get a player's rating card for every casino you play in and always use it.*

Becoming a "known" player at the casinos you favor can get you little extras that you might not otherwise deserve. At the old Bally's Grand in Atlantic City [now the Hilton], the beautiful A.P. and I were supposed to have a free room for two nights during midweek in February. When we checked in, the hostess told us that they were upgrading our room to a full suite. I asked her how come. She said that the suites were empty for that night and, "as a reward for your patronage," they were upgrading some of their comped players to suites. It was a magnificent suite with spectacular ocean views, a jacuzzi, a bar, a huge television. At that time, I was rated a $20 player at blackjack!

2. *Get a player's rating card for casinos you don't play in.*

Sometimes casinos offer special deals to card members regardless of whether they have used their cards recently or played there at all. I have a box filled with players' cards from just about every casino I've ever visited. In their off-seasons, I'll be invited to spend a few days at their properties free or at radically reduced rates—and guess what? In some of these places I've never even placed a bet! Simply having a rating card puts you on the casinos' mailing lists and all casino mailings have one thing in common—they are giving you something to get you to come to their properties. Sometimes it's as small as a pin or a pen, sometimes it's as big as a car or a house!

3. *Never play one second at any game until you've handed the floor person your player's rating card.*

You want every second of your time recorded to maximize your comps. Sometimes casino floorpeople can get a little lazy. Sometimes they have so many people playing that they might overlook a new player as they hustle and bustle through their chores. That new player then makes several bets but does not get comp credit for them. Remember, don't place a single bet until it counts for your rating. In the new games, where you are facing tough odds, you want your rating to be as accurate as possible. (Or, if it is inaccurate, you want it to be inaccurate in your favor!)

4. *Don't be afraid to sit out a hand or two every so often especially if the pit person is not watching the game closely.*

Most times the pit person rating you won't notice or won't care. You'll be getting comp time for time when your money is not at risk. Time is money for the casino. Time is also money for the player who can get that time recorded as playing time while he isn't playing! Sitting out a hand or two every now and then is a wonderful way to squeeze a little extra from the casino comp department.

5. *Learn to play the games perfectly.*

Most raters are too busy to really analyze your play and you will often receive a "typical" rating and get much more in comps than your level of expertise actually deserves. Here's a really good thing about the new games described in this book. Just about everyone who plays them plays them abysmally. Most of the casinos rating players rate them based on this poor play profile. In fact, there are actually pit people who don't know that good strategies have now been developed for the new games. Play those good strategies but get a "typical" rating and it's comp points in the bank!

6. *Pool your comps with your spouse or friend(s).*

People who combine their comps can often get much more. Most dinner comps are for two people. Most show comps are also for two people. Most room comps are, yes, for two people. In the comp kingdom, two can live as cheaply as one. Happily, the reverse is not true. Two do not get the comps of one. If you and a spouse, or you and a friend, make it known that you wish to pool your comps, many casino hosts will allow this. You will now increase the value of the comps that you get. For example, instead of the cafe, which your play alone can get for two, you will get gourmet for two, which the combined play of you and yours merits.

7. *The moment you ask for a comp, stop playing.*

Many casinos love to keep players waiting for comps in the hope that the players will keep playing and lose more money. I have seen this scenario a thousand times: A somewhat low-rolling player asks for a comp and the floorperson then disappears, ostensibly to find out from some higher authority if the player warrants a comp. The player foolishly continues to play until the floorperson comes back with an answer. "Sorry," says the floorperson, "you have to play for fifteen more minutes."

"But I just played another fifteen minutes," says the player.

"Oh, I'll check again," says the floorperson, who again vanishes.

Fifteen minutes later, the floorperson appears with a comp. The player has played an extra half hour to get that comp.

When you ask for a comp, stop playing. If you can, however, stay seated at the table. The casino might want to free up your chair and this alone can speed up the processing of your comp.

8. *Always cash in for more than you intend to play with.*

Casino raters will make a note of how much you cashed in for and the casino will assume that you are willing to lose that amount. In close comp calls, they will refer to your buy-in to give them a handle on how much they should buy *you*.

9. *Be friendly to the dealers and the pit crew.*

The granting of comps, although based on a formula, is not a science. The formula is merely a guide. Casino pit crews have to deal with a lot of boorish players and a friendly face will often get them to give a comp that is slightly more valuable than the friendly face's action actually deserved. You might bet $10 on one hand and on the next bet $25. A friendly rater will record the $25 and not the $10 wager.

10. *Be aware that no comp is worth losing money or sleep over.*

A true player plays to win money, not to impress his or her spouse, or the pit crew. Just play the games you have decided to play perfectly and the comps will take care of themselves.

One last comp hint. If you are betting $25 or more at any of the new games, it's a good thing to make the acquaintance of a host at your favorite casinos. Often hosts have the power to give you comps that the pit crew can't give. They have what is called "the power of the pen." They also have much more latitude in the granting of comps than do the floor people, as they can take into consideration other factors besides your play: for example, do you bring friends who play with you to the casino? Are you one of a group of people that the particular host knows? Sometimes it is as simple as the host liking you. People who have to deal with the public take a bit of a battering every day on the job. They appreciate those players who flatter rather than batter them for comps.

9

In Their Own Words: Voices from the World of New Games

You now know everything you need to know in order to play the strongest possible strategies, which are also the best practical strategies against the new casino card games Caribbean Stud, Let It Ride, and Three Card Poker. The Bold Card Play strategies will serve you well. Yet, in the interests of completeness, I have decided to use this chapter to allow those involved with these games—from creators, to writers, to players—to have their say in their own words. First we'll hear from a heavyweight gaming corporation, the Minnesota-based Shuffle Master, highlighting their company's rationale for exisiting and why they created Let It Ride.

...in 1982, ...John Breeding, a long haul truck driver from Minnesota, envisioned a gadget that would shuffle playing cards. The idea was sparked from an article he read in The Wall Street Journal *describing Atlantic City's frustration with card counters at casino blackjack tables. Breeding was convinced that a device that could shuffle decks of cards between hands would thwart card counters and be embraced by the casino industry, and he set out to design one.*

Almost ten years later...Breeding and his company, Shuffle Master, Inc., had its first automatic card shuffler licensed by the state of Nevada. Today, Shuffle Master shufflers can be found in nearly 400 casinos around the world.

While Shuffle Master currently offers a variety of shufflers including single deck, and multiple deck models, Breeding's original version was a single deck shuffler for which there was limited applications. To stimulate a larger demand for the single deck shuffler [italics mine], Breeding invented Let It Ride, a table game based on five card stud poker.

Press release from Shuffle Master

The machines give me a headache and I don't want to play blackjack. I don't like the fact that people always watch what you're doing and comment on how you play. I like Three Card Poker because I get a chance to win big. I also get to play my hands the way I want to play them without anyone commenting on it. I like the bonus part, too. I think the game gives you a good chance to win if you make the right decisions on your cards. I like it more than the machines and much more than blackjack. I hope it catches on.

Christine L., player, Memphis, TN

1. *A Caribbean Stud player will have more units in action than a Let-It-Ride player. The reason is that a Caribbean Stud player calls the dealer more than half of the time, whereas a Let-It-Ride player lets his wagers ride only 15.43% of the time. A caution is in order here: Do not regard more units in action as equivalent to more winnings.*
2. *A Let-It-Ride player can win a much larger amount than a Caribbean Stud player due to the more liberal payout schedule, higher maximum aggregate payout and the higher tournament [now bonus] prize....*

3. *A Caribbean Stud player will receive a winning hand more frequently than a Let-It-Ride player.*

4. *A Caribbean Stud player will receive a lower average payoff on his winning hands than a Let-It-Ride player.*

5. *When losing a hand, a Caribbean Stud player loses 0.4437 more units than a Let-It-Ride player on average.*

6. *A Let-It-Ride player will experience broader bankroll fluctuations than a Caribbean Stud player.*

7. *A Caribbean Stud player will lose more than a Let-It-Ride player in the long run due to the higher casino advantage.*

8. *A Let-It-Ride player can take back two of his initial three bet units.*

There is no intention nor need to conclude here which game is better, since players of either game will be losers in the long run anyway. However, Caribbean Stud does have much room for improvement. First, players' aversion to the 'Dealer must have an Ace-King or higher to qualify' rule definitely is a major impediment to the game's continued popularity. Second, more liberal payouts should be offered. Frequent losses won't bring the players back....

Stanley Ko, in *Mastering the Game of Caribbean Stud Poker*

I'm quitting. I played this game [Caribbean Stud] on a cruise ship the first time and I won a lot of money and I thought that it was better than all the other games. I was wrong. I was really wrong. I haven't won a damn thing since that cruise. That must have been a fluke, just beginner's luck. I like the way the game is played and all, but I can single-handedly put all the dealers' kids through school with what I've lost. I think it must have a huge house edge for the casino. I really don't know anyone who's won at it, although I was at a table when someone hit a straight flush.

Samuel S., player, New York, New York

...readers must recognize that all gambling games involve a consider-able element of luck and that in the short run, winning or losing may depend more on luck than expert strategy. But, over the long haul, expert strategy will produce the best results for you.

Lenny Frome, in *Expert Strategy for Let It Ride*

From our first-hand experience in Las Vegas casinos, we have seen players floundering around with this game [Caribbean Stud]. There is no consensus regarding the strategy and the dealers and the pit bosses can offer no useful assistance. This confusion must translate into losses for the play-ers.

Ira. D. Frome and Elliot A. Frome, in
Expert Strategy for Caribbean Stud Poker

Blackjack bites it. All those experts, all those books, and I've never known a single person who has won in the long run. Do you know anyone who really wins at the game? It's all bull. So you study a million different hands and what to do and you still end up getting your ass kicked. Why do that? I like Let It Ride because you don't have to really memorize a lot of strategies and you have a chance to take home some big money. So what if all the writers tell me that it's a losing game—they're all losing games for cry-ing out loud. Who's kidding who, huh?

Danny P., player, Brooklyn, New York

Every time the casino brings in a new game I play it. I'm a new game tryer. I just can't seem to find the perfect game for me. It's like trying on clothes. At first you like them and then you get tired of them and want to buy

new clothes. I've played roulette. I've played craps and blackjack and Caribbean Stud. I've played slots and video poker. I don't think I won once at video poker. Right now my favorite is Three Card Poker, which I play in Tunica all the time. I've had some pretty good luck with it. It seems to give the players a better chance than the other games I've played.

Jill P., player, Paragould, Arkansas

Mathematically, about 75 percent of the hands dealt to you in Let It Ride will result in no-win—a surprise to many poker players who assume that tens or better aren't that hard to catch. It is not uncommon to be dealt many hands in a row and not win anything. This means that your playing bankroll will be diminishing until you get lucky and are dealt one of the payoff hands. When this occurs, you better be ready to take your profits and run.

Henry Tamburin, in *The Experts' Guide to Casino Games*

Three Card Poker is a lot of fun. I used to play the machines but they were getting boring after awhile. And I wanted to talk to other people. I get that at Three Card Poker. The other night I had a great run of cards and I made over a thousand dollars. I never did that on the machines.

Mary J., player, Memphis, Tennessee

Anyone that has ever read books about casino gambling knows that there are three basic steps to becoming a winning player at any game offered: (1) The player must learn the rules of the game. (2) The player must learn the correct strategy required to improve his chances of winning. (3) The

player must learn how to manage his money so that he can last through periods of losing and be able to take advantage of periods of winning.

Walter Thomason, in *The Experts' Guide to Casino Games*

What is the point of playing in a casino? It's for fun and sometimes taking these strategies that you write about too seriously takes away the fun. If you can't really win, then why bother to figure out the odds? In the end, it's a losing proposition from the economic standpoint. The difference in following a predetermined strategy or playing as the mood hits you is not so great in the short run. I go to the casinos three times a year. I bring $2,000 and when that's gone, I'm done. That's all there is to it. I play the new games because I figure that's the cutting edge. Have I ever won? Not really. You can't win, so why ask me if I've ever won? If people are fooled into thinking they can win they will spend quality time trying to figure out ways to win. It's much better to accept the fact that it's a loser—casino gambling is a loser—and ...You know, I've kinda forgotten what your question was.

Professor Edwin S., player, San Francisco, California

When you play in a casino, you want to have a good time that is free from guilt, shame, or fear....If at any time you begin to lose concentration, get tired, experience panic or anger, leave the table and only resume play when you're back to your calm, lovable self. Remember that most casinos are open twenty-four hours a day. They won't go away if you get some sleep or have a meal. The statistical odds are already against you; why add to your worries with a mind that is not working at full efficiency?

Miron Stablinsky and Jeremy Silman, in
Zen and the Art of Casino Gaming

Just because [the] House has the advantage does not mean you are destined to fall prey to it all the time. Let's say your expected average hourly loss rate is $10 in some hypothetical casino game. You find that sometimes you do much better and sometimes you do much worse. You just won't lose exactly $10 every hour you play. As a matter of fact it is unlikely for your hourly loss rate to dutifully perform what it's supposed to perform for a short period of time. In the short run the results seldom conform to the theoretical norm. These fluctuations in the expected results are measured by statisticians as standard deviation, and for all practical purposes your results will be within three standard deviations of your expectation. For example, if the standard deviation is $20 per hour, at a risk level of three standard deviations you could be ahead as much as $20 x 3 - $10 = $50 or behind as much as $20 x 3 + $10 = $70 in one hour of play despite that your average hourly loss rate is a mere $10. Your expectation remains unchanged but it is merely the standard deviation that dominates the results.

Stanley Ko, in *Mastering the Game of Let it Ride*

I believe absolutely in limiting one's losses with an absolute loss-limit (the session stake) but I don't believe you should limit your potential for a big win. A win limit should be somewhat flexible to allow for a potential economic killing.

Alene Paone, in *The Experts' Guide to Casino Games*

What a perfect game for the casinos of the world; one that combines elements of 5-card Stud Poker with slot machines. Does it get any better than this? You can actually play a real game of poker and at the same time try for a giant jackpot like those offered by various banks of progressive slot machines; jackpots that can easily reach over $100,000. ...Yes, anyone who knows the ranking of poker hands can attack [Caribbean Stud]. And those

who have played 5-card Stud Poker will find this game to be a snap. However, as is the case with most casino games, the casino has a large, virtually unbeatable edge.

Dennis R. Harrison, *Win at the Casino*

I will finish with a description by Derek Webb, the inventor of Three Card Poker, of the background to the game and then one about Derek Webb and his invention of it.

A few hundred years ago, in the time of Shakespeare, Queen Elizabeth I and Henry VIII, the British played a betting game called Primero. Each player had three cards and could win with the highest numerical total, the highest card, the highest pair or the highest three of a kind.

With time the numerical value aspect disappeared and the name changed to Post-and-Pair, describing the winning bet features. As the betting rounds became more significant, Wild Cards were introduced called Braggers and the name of the game changed yet again to Brag.

Although there is a reference to [American] Generals playing Brag before a Civil War battle, the name Brag had generally disappeared [from America] with the British after the Revolution. In common with other poker derivative games, the straight, flush, and straight flush were added to three card rankings and the game split into a variety of forms and names throughout the States.

All these games, such as Guts, Survival, Texas Western, Three Toed Pete, and Three Card Ante have the common feature of fast, exciting action with only three cards.

Press release by Derek Webb

Three Card Poker was invented by Derek Webb, a successful poker player based in Britain. When Derek visited Vegas with his British friends,

they played the poker derivative games available, but found them to be slow and boring. Derek was aware that the British Casino Association wanted to introduce new games and felt that having invented versions of poker for dealers' choice games, he could invent a new poker game for the British casinos.

It was immediately obvious that the best game to base the new game on would be Brag, which is still played in Britain. Derek set to designing a game that had the attractive aspects of the original historical game with the multiple win opportunities and providing a choice of play modes, part of the appeal of craps and roulette.

The game was initially shown to the casino industry as Casino Brag, and whilst this name was acceptable in the first European location, American operators wanted something different.

Three Card Poker was the best choice as it describes exactly and simply what the game is. This was confirmed in a player survey conducted by Prime Table Games, Webb's marketing vehicle.

It is ironic that the game invented for Britain is still waiting to be introduced there.... However, in the British offshore island Isle of Man Casino, the game is now more popular than blackjack. The first U.S. state to approve Three Card Poker was Mississippi, where it now is played in most casinos. Here the game is so popular that the statewide action on Three Card Poker exceeds that on established poker derivatives such as Pai Gow, Let it Ride, and Caribbean Stud. Again, in the limited stakes market of Colorado and South Dakota, Three Card Poker is more popular than Let it Ride....

Webb says: "Players can quickly see how fair and easy to play Three Card Poker is, while also being very exciting and sociable. I've got real lucky to hit on a game that is going to be a natural winner in the fight for space on the casino floor."

Press release by Prime Table Games

Glossary

Ace: The highest card in poker.

Action: The total amount a player bets over time at a given casino game. Used as a standard of judgment for casino comps.

Action Player: A player who bets big and/or plays the highest house-edge bets. Sometimes used as a euphemism for "dumb" player.

Anchor: The player who sits to the right of the dealer and is the last to act on his hand. Sometimes referred to as the "third base-man."

Ante: Any initial or opening bet to start a game. Technical name for the opening bet in Three Card Poker and Caribbean Stud.

Bank: The person who covers a bet in a game. In most casino games, the bank is the casino itself. Also, one of the three bets at bac-carat.

Bankroll: The total amount of money a player has that is used for gambling.

Basic Strategy: In blackjack, the best possible play of any player hand against any dealer up-card. In other games, the best play available.

Bet: The space where the player calls the dealer in Caribbean Stud. Also, name for any wager at any game.

Bet blind: To bet without seeing your cards.

Bias: The tendency of a game to favor either the dealer or the player over an extended period of time.

Black action: A bet made with a black ($100) chip.

Blacks: Chips valued at $100.

Bluff: An attempt to take the pot by making players think you have a better hand than you actually do. Staying in on hands that you should fold in Caribbean Stud, Let it Ride, or Three Card Poker.

Body time: For purposes of comping, how much time your body has been at the table. Some of this time, you will not have money at risk.

Bold Card Play: The set of strategies designed specifically for Caribbean Stud, Let It Ride and Three Card Poker that will reduce the casinos' edge against the players.

Bonus: A special payment for select hands at all the new games.

Break down a bet: Separate chips by the various denominations. Used by dealers to accurately pay off bets.

Bull: Another name for the ace in poker.

Buy in: Exchanging cash for chips at a table. The original amount of cash exchanged for chips in the beginning of a player's action.

Cage: The cashier's area of the casino where chips are exchanged for cash.

Call: To continue to play by putting up extra money.

Card: Also referred to as a *player rating card* or *comp card*, the plastic card that looks like a credit card that casinos use to keep track of a player's action.

Card counting: Keeping track of the cards that have been played or are in the other players' hands in order to gain an edge over casino and/or to determine the best strategy for the playing of one's hand. Effective in blackjack but only a theoretical possibility at the new games.

Casino manager: The person responsible for seeing that the various games of the casino are handled properly.

Centerfield: The middle betting position at the center of a table that has seven players.

Chasing losses: Increasing your bets in order to recoup what you've lost. A very dangerous way to play.

Checks: Another name for chips.

Choppy game: A game where neither the house nor the player has been winning consistently. Opposite of a streak.

Clocking: Keeping track of the results of a given game to determine how or whether to bet.

Cold table: Any table where you have been losing.

Color up: To exchange smaller denomination chips for larger denomination chips at the table.

Comp: Stands for complementary. Casinos give certain inducements such as free and discounted rooms, food, and shows for certain levels and durations of play.

Credit line: The amount of credit that a casino will extend to a player.

Credit manager: The person responsible for who gets credit and for how much.

Crew: The personnel who work a game.

Crimp: A bend in a card put there by a player or dealer for identification purposes. A cheating technique.

Crossroader: A casino cheat.

Cut the deck: To divide the deck before dealing. Often done by a player.

Daub: To cheat at cards by placing a small amount of paint or ink on the card for the purposes of later identifying it.

Dead hand: A hand that can no longer be made. A hand that has been discarded.

Dead table: A table where no one is playing.

Dealer: The casino employee who staffs the games offered. The person who distributes the cards.

Deuces: The two-valued cards.

Drop Box: The box hanging from the table where the players' cash is deposited after exchanging it for chips.

Even money: A wager the winning of which pays off at one to one. That is, if you bet one dollar, you win one dollar. In the casino an "even-money" bet does not mean that the odds are actually 50-50.

Face cards: The King, Queen and Jack. Also known as *picture cards.*

False cut: A cut of the cards that leaves them in the same order that they were in as before.

Fair game: A game where neither the casino nor the player has the edge.

Favorable deck: A deck whose remaining cards favor the player.

First base: The seat at the table immediately to the dealer's left.

Flat bet: A bet that is paid off at even money or a bet that is the same amount hand after hand.

Floorman (floorperson): The individual responsible for supervising several tables in a pit.

Fluctuation in probability: Numbers or hands appearing out of all proportion to their probability. A short sequence that favors the house or the player. A mathematical term that is translated as good or bad luck depending on whether the fluctuation favors the player or the house.

Flush: Any five cards of the same suit. For example: two, four, six, eight, and ten, all diamonds.

Fold: To drop out of play.

Four flush: Four of the same suit. A four-flusher is someone who attempted to win the pot by declaring a flush when he only had four of the same suit.

Four-of-a-kind: Any four cards of the same denomination. For example: four Kings.

Four straight: Four cards in sequence.

Fun book: Coupon book used by the casinos to encourage play. Also contains discounts for drinks, food, novelties, et cetera.

Full house: Three of a kind and a pair.

Gambling stake: Amount of money reserved for gambling. Same as bankroll.

George: A good tipper.

Glim: A concealed mirror used for cheating at cards.

Grand martingale: A wagering system where you double your bet and add one extra unit after a loss.

Greens: Chips valued at $25.

Grifter: A scam artist.

Grind: A derogatory term for a small roller. A player who bets small amounts. The term used to descibe what the casino edge does to a player's bankroll.

Hand mucking: A casino dealer who palms and then substitutes cards into a game at the appropriate time.

Head-to-head: To play against the dealer with no other players in the game. Sometimes referred to as *heads up* or *face-to-face* or *one-on-one.*

High card: In hands with no pairs or better, the highest denomination card will win.

High roller: A player who plays for large stakes.

Hold: The actual amount the casinos take from their games.

Host: The person responsible for seeing that high rollers are treated with the dignity and graciousness their wallets merit.

Hot and cold system: A wager on the side that won previously. Another name for the streak method of betting.

Hot table: A table where the players have been winning.

House edge: The advantage, usually expressed as a percentage, that the casino has over the player at a given game. This advantage is usually attained by not paying back the correct odds on a wager or by structuring games so that the casino wins more decisions than the players. Sometimes the edge is a combination of both.

House odds: The payoff that reflects the casino's tax on your winning bet.

House person: A dealer who is unusually concerned with the casino's profits. A dealer who enjoys watching the players lose. A dealer who identifies with the casino. Sometimes derogatorily referred to as the *house pet* or *house plant.*

Hustler: A gambling cheat.

Inside straight: A straight that can only be completed by drawing a card that is between the highest and lowest denomination in the sequence. For example: two, three, five, six can only be completed by drawing a four.

Irregularity: A departure from the standard procedures at a given game. What players might suffer from when they've lost more than they can afford to.

Jackpot: A grand payout for hitting a certain premium hand.

Joker: A wild card that can usually be substituted for any card in the deck. Usually resembles a court jester.

Juice: The percent the casino takes out of a winning bet. Also the name for any commission charged on a bet either before or after winning it. A person with pull in the casino.

Junket: A trip organized and subsidized by a casino to bring gamblers to play at the games.

Kibitzer: An individual who is not playing at a given game but is giving unwanted advice.

Laydown: Another name for a bet. Also, someone who quits in the middle of a game.

Layout: The design imprinted with the various bets of a given game.

Level: An honest game.

Long end of the bet: The side that must pay off more than it collects.

Long run: The concept that a player could play so often that probability would tend to even out. That is, you would start to see the total appearance of decisions or events approximating what probability theory predicts. A "long-run" player is one who plays a lot!

Marker: The check the player fills out before receiving credit at a casino table. A promissory note or I.O.U.

Martingale system of wagering: Doubling one's bet after a loss in an attempt to make back all your losses and a small win. Dangerous.

Money plays: The call that alerts the dealer and the pit that the player is betting cash and not chips.

Mucker: Anyone who uses slight-of-hand techniques to cheat at cards or other games.

Negative progression: Any system of wagering where you increase bets after a loss.

Nickel: Five dollar chips—usually red.

No action: A call made by a dealer that the casino will not cover a particular bet or that a particular deal doesn't count.

On the square: A game that is honest.

Open: To make the first bet.

Openers: The cards that qualify a player or, in Caribbean Stud and Three Card Poker, the cards that qualify a dealer.

Overbetting: Betting more than your bankroll or your psychology can handle.

Outside straight: A straight that can be completed by adding a card at one end. For example: an outside straight that is ace, two, three, four can only be completed by a five.

Open-ended straight: A straight that can be completed at either end of the sequence. An outside straight that is two, three, four, five is "open-ended" because it can be completed with an ace or a six.

Paddle: The tool used to push the money into the drop box.

Paint: A picture card.

Pair: Two cards of one denomination. For example: two aces.

Pair Plus: The separate wager in the noncompetitive part of Three Card Poker that pays bonuses for a pair or better.

Pat hand: Any hand in a card game that does not require getting additional cards.

P.C.: The house edge expressed as a percentage.

Pinching: Illegally removing chips from one's bet after an unfavorable decision.

Pit: An area in the casino consisting of a number of table games.

Pit Boss: The individual in charge of a pit.

Power of the pen: The ability on the part of some casino executives to issue hotel comps to players.

Premium players: A casino term meaning big bettors or players with big credit lines.

Progressive jackpot: A jackpot that continues to increase as players play until one player hits the necessary hand to win it.

Prop: Another name for a *shill*. A person employed by the casino to play a game to generate action. Most often used in baccarat and poker.

Push: Casinoese for a tie where neither the player nor the casino wins the bet.

Qualify: The rule that mandates that a dealer receive a certain minimum hand for the game to continue or for the competition to begin.

Quarters: Chips valued at $25—usually green.

Rating: Evaluating a player's play for the purpose of determining comps.

Rating card: The card used for rating the player.

Reds: Casino chips worth five dollars.

Riffle: Splitting the deck in two and shuffling both sections into each other.

RFB: Stands for room, food and beverage. The highest level of comps that a player can get. Includes free rooms, free meals, shows, parties, limos, and sometimes even plane fare.

Royal flush: The highest hand composed of an Ace, King, Queen, Jack and ten of the same suit.

Rule card: The card that explains the rules for a given game.

Rush: A quick winning streak.

Scam: Any scheme to defraud a casino or player.

Scared money: Money that you are betting with that you can't afford to lose.

Session: A predetermined or given period of time or money won/lost or number of decisions that a player uses to establish when to play and when to go.

Session Stake: The amount of money a player has set aside for a given period of play. Usually a percentage of the total bankroll.

Shift boss: The individual in charge of a casino during a given work shift.

Shill: See *Prop*.

Short end of a bet: The side of the bet that has to pay off less than it will win.

Short odds: Anything that is less than the true odds payoff of a bet.

Short run: The limited amount of time during any given session when probability theory will seemingly be skewered by streaks and fluctuations.

Side bet: A second bet, in addition to the normal bet(s), on a proposition at a table game. The bonus and jackpot bets that require an extra dollar to play in Let it Ride and Caribbean Stud.

Soft players: A term for poor players.

Spread: The difference between the minimum and the maximum bet that a player makes at a given game.

Stacked deck: A deck of cards that has been prearranged in a certain order for cheating purposes.

Stiff: A bad hand.

Straight: Any five cards in order of denomination. For example, five, six, seven, eight and nine composed of various suits.

Straight Flush: Any five cards in order of the same suit. For example, five, six, seven, eight, and nine of hearts.

Sweat: Casino personnel who get upset when a player is winning are said to "sweat" their games. Also, a player who is losing and is worried.

Table hopping: Moving from table to table in a casino.

Take down: To remove a bet before a decision is made.

TARGET: Controversial method of selecting a table at which to play in blackjack.

Tell: Any unconscious signal that allows you to know what another player or the dealer has in his or her hand.

Third base: The position to the dealer's right. Player who acts last on his hand.

Three flush: Three cards to a flush.

Three-of-a-kind: Three cards of the same denomination. For example: three nines.

Three straight: Three cards to a straight.

Toke: Another term for a tip for a dealer.

Toke hustler: A dealer who tries to get the players to tip him.

Tom: Casinoese for a poor tipper.

Topping the deck: Palming cards for the purpose of cheating.

True odds: The actual probability of an event happening.

Two pair: Two cards of one denomination and two cards of another denomination. For example, two sixes and two queens.

Underground joint: An illegal casino.

Unfavorable deck: A deck or shoe that favors the casino over the player.

Up card: Any card that is dealt face up.

Vic: Sucker.

Vig or vigorish: The casino tax on a bet. The amount taken out of a player's winning wager or the amount of the commission paid on a wager.

Virgin principle: The superstition that a beginner will have good luck. Also known as *beginner's luck.*

Wash: One bet cancels out another bet. Also, the process of mixing fresh cards together on the top of the table without lifting them.

Wild card: A card that can be used for any other card in the game.

Zero: A loser.

INDEX

OTHER BEST-SELLING GAMBLING BOOKS BY FRANK SCOBLETE

Beat the Craps out of the Casinos
ISBN 0-929387-34-1

Best Blackjack
ISBN 1-56625-057-9

Break the One-Armed Bandits
ISBN 1-56625-001-3

Guerrilla Gambling
ISBN 1-56625-027-7

Spin Roulette Gold
ISBN 1-56625-074-9

Victory at Video Poker
ISBN 1-56625-043-9

Books are available from:

Bonus Books, Inc.
160 E. Illinois Street
Chicago, IL 60611
phone: (312) 467-0580, or call toll-free (800) 225-3775
fax: (312) 467-9271

Visit our website at http: // www.bonus-books.com